Loftus Surname

Ireland: 1600s to 1900s

From Ireland Church Records of Baptism, Marriage and Death

Comprised of Roman Catholic and Church of Ireland Records

From Counties Carlow, Cork, Kerry and Dublin City

Compiled by **Donovan Hurst**

April 11, 2013

ISBN: 1939958199
ISBN-13: 978-1-939958-19-8

Dedication

This work is dedicated to all of those that came before us and shaped our lives to make us the people that we are today.

Table of Contents

Introduction

This is a compilation of individuals who have the surname of Loftus that lived in the country of Ireland from the 1600s to the 1900s. I have placed each entry into one of four categories: Families, Individual Births/Baptisms, Individual Burials, and Individual Marriages. If a marriage entry primarily concerns an Individual Loftus whom is female, then I have placed that entry under the category of Individual Marriages. If a marriage entry primarily concerns an Individual Loftus whom is male, then I have placed that entry under the category of Families. Images of many of these listings are available at

http://churchrecords.irishgenealogy.ie/churchrecords/.

To help guide the reader of this work, the format of this book is as follows:

- Main Family Entry (Husband and Wife) (Father and Mother)

  o Child of Main Family Entry, including Spouse(s) when available

    ▪ Grandchild of Main Family Entry, including Spouse(s) when available

      • Great-Grandchild of Main Family Entry, including Spouse(s) when available

(**Bolded Text**) following any entry includes any additional information such as Residence(s), Occupation(s), Signature(s), etc. when available.

Hurst

Some of the fonts used in this work symbolizes Celtic writing. The traditional letters, numbers, and punctuation marks and their Celtic counterparts are as follows:

Traditional Letters (Uppercase & Lowercase)

A a B b C c D d E f G g H h I i J j K k L l M m N n O o P p Q q R r S s T t U u V v W w X x Y y Z z

Celtic Letters (Uppercase & Lowercase)

A a B b C c D ð E e F ꝼ G g H h I í J j K k L l M m

N n O o P p Q q R ꞧ S s T t U u V ʋ W ꞷ X x Y ʒ Z z

Traditional Numbers

1 2 3 4 5 6 7 8 9 10

Celtic Numbers

1 2 3 4 5 6 7 8 9 10

Traditional Punctuation

. , : ' " & - ( )

Celtic Punctuation

. , : ' " & - ( )

Parish Churches

Carlow (Church of Ireland)

Aghold Parish, Bilboa Parish, Carlow Parish, Clonmelsh Parish, Dunleckney Parish, Kiltennel Parish, Tullow Parish, and Urglin Parish.

Cork & Ross

(Roman Catholic or RC)

Cork - South Parish and Cork - SS. Peter & Paul Parish.

Dublin (Church of Ireland)

Arbour Hill Barracks Parish, Clondalkin Parish, Glasnevin Parish, Kilmainham Parish, Lucan Parish, Richmond Barracks Parish, Rotunda Chapel Parish, St. Anne Parish, St. Catherine Parish, St. George Parish, St. John Parish, St. Luke Parish, St. Mark Parish, St. Mary Parish, St. Matthias Parish, St. Michan Parish, St. Nicholas Without Parish, St. Paul Parish, St. Peter Parish, St. Stephen Parish, St. Thomas Parish, St. Werburgh Parish, and Taney Parish.

Dublin (Roman Catholic or RC)

Harrington Street Parish, Rathmines Parish, Sandyford Parish, SS. Michael & John Parish, St. Andrew Parish, St. Audoen Parish, St. Catherine Parish, St. James Parish, St. Mary Parish, St. Mary, Donnybrook Parish, St. Mary, Haddington Road Parish, St. Mary, Pro Cathedral Parish, St. Michan Parish, and St. Nicholas Parish.

Kerry (Roman Catholic or RC)

Dromod Parish, Killarney Parish, and Tralee.

Families

- Adam Loftus, bur. 8 Apr 1605 (Burial, **St. Patrick Parish**) & Jane Purdon, bur. 21 Jul 1595 (Burial, **St. Patrick Parish**)
  - Unknown Loftus (Son)
  - Edward Loftus, bur. 5 Sep 1602 (Burial, **St. Patrick Parish**) & Anne Duke, d. 6 Jul 1601, bur. 7 Jul 1601 (Burial, **St. Patrick Parish**)

Edward Loftus (son):

Social Status - Sir, Knight

Remarks about Death - The church register states the following

for the year 1602:

"Edward Loftus, the Queen's Sergeant, "the Lord

Chancellor's brother's eldest son," bur. Sept. 5 [F.]

Anne Duke, daughter of Henry Duke (daughter-in-law):

Place of Burial - Loftus Vault - July 7, 1601

Henry Duke (father):

Social Status - Knight

Hurst

- o Unknown Loftus (Son)

- o Thomas Loftus – d. 12 Dec 1635, bur. 14 Dec 1635 (Burial, **St. Patrick Parish**)

Thomas Loftus (son):

Residence - Timocho, Queen's County - December 12, 1635

Social Status - Knight

Place of Burial - Loftus Vault - December 14, 1635

Adam Loftus (father):

Occupation - Archbishop of Dublin

Place of Burial - Loftus Vault - April 8, 1605

Jane Purdon (mother):

Place of Burial - "in the Loftus vault on the South side of the high altar"

- July 21, 1595

- Adam Loftus & Penelope Street – 21 Feb 1651 (Marriage, **St. John Parish**)

- Adam Loftus & Unknown

- o Lettice Loftus, d. 26 Oct 1633, bur. 29 Oct 1633 (Burial, **St. Patrick Parish**) & Richard Parsons

Adam Loftus (father):

Residence - Rathfarnham - October 29, 1633

Social Status - Sir

Loftus Surname Ireland: 1600s to 1900s

- Adam Viscount Loftus & Unknown

  o Robert Loftus – d. 11 Oct 1640, bur. 16 Oct 1640 (Burial, **St. Patrick Parish**)

Robert Loftus (son):

Place of Burial - "in the Choir" - October 16, 1640

Adam Viscount Loftus (father):

Residence - Ely - October 16, 1640

- Alfred Loftus & Emma Jane Unknown

  o Albert George Loftus – b. 8 Sep 1872, bapt. 14 Nov 1872 (Baptism, **Richmond Barracks Parish**)

Alfred Loftus (father):

Residence - Richmond Barracks - November 14, 1872

Occupation - Color Sergeant, 97th Regiment - November 14, 1872

- Arthur Loftus & Anne Unknown

  o Edward Loftus – bapt. 23 Oct 1679 (Baptism, **St. Michan Parish**)

Arthur Loftus (father):

Occupation - Esquire - October 23, 1679

Hurst

- Arthur Loftus & Unknown

  o Jane Grey Loftus & James Cuffe St. George – 15 May 1856 (Marriage, **St. Peter Parish**)

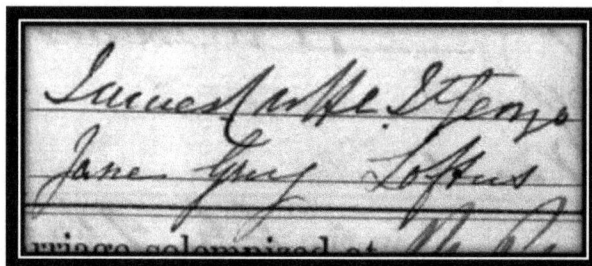

Signatures:

Jane Grey Loftus (daughter):

   Residence - 66 Lower Baggot Street - May 15, 1856

James Cuffe St. George, son of Richard Bligh St. George (son-in-law):

   Residence - 134 Great Brunswick Street - May 15, 1856

   Occupation - Esquire - May 15, 1856

Richard Bligh St. George (father):

   Occupation - Bart

Arthur Loftus (father):

   Occupation - Captain, Royal Navy

Loftus Surname Ireland: 1600s to 1900s

Wedding Witnesses:

J. E. St. George & Arthur Loftus

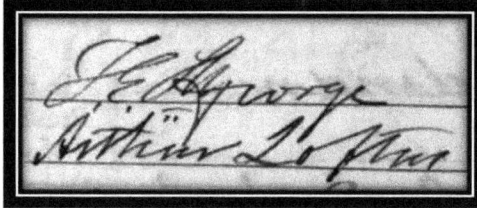

Signatures:

- Con Loftus & Lucy Loftus

  o Mary Loftus – bapt. 30 May 1826 (Baptism, **St. Mary. Pro Cathedral Parish (RC)**)

Con Loftus (father):

Residence - Cole's Lane - May 30 1826

- David Loftus & Bridget Gibbons

  o William Loftus – b. 18 Mar 1866, bapt. 2 Apr 1866 (Baptism, **St. Nicholas Parish (RC)**)

David Loftus (father):

Residence - 46 New Market - April 2, 1866

- David Loftus & Bridget Unknown

  o Patrick Loftus & Anne Byrne (B y r n e) – 23 Jan 1876 (Marriage, **St. Andrew Parish (RC)**)

    ▪ Bridget Loftus – b. 1877, bapt. 1877 (Baptism, **St. Andrew Parish (RC)**)

    ▪ Esther Anne Loftus – b. 1878, bapt. 1878 (Baptism, **St. Andrew Parish (RC)**)

    ▪ Patrick Loftus – b. 1879, bapt. 1879 (Baptism, **St. Andrew Parish (RC)**)

Hurst

Patrick Loftus (son):

Residence - Corey Lane, Drumcondra - January 23, 1876

19 Mark Street - 1877

1878

1879

Anne Byrne, daughter of William Byrne & Bridget Unknown (daughter-in-law):

Residence - 208 Great Brunswick Street - January 23, 1876

Wedding Witnesses:

Andrew Byrne & Catherine Harvey

- o Mary Loftus & Peter Lee – 3 Feb 1879 (Marriage, **St. Andrew Parish** (RC))
  - ▪ Mary Bridget Lee – b. 1 Mar 1880, bapt. 2 Mar 1880 (Baptism, **St. Agatha Parish** (RC))
  - ▪ David Lee – b. 10 Dec 1881, bapt. 13 Dec 1881 (Baptism, **St. Agatha Parish** (RC))
  - ▪ Peter Paul Lee – b. 18 Oct 1883, bapt. 23 Oct 1883 (Baptism, **St. Agatha Parish** (RC))

Mary Loftus (daughter):

Residence - 19 Mark Street - February 3, 1879

Peter Lee, son of John Lee & Mary Unknown (son-in-law):

Residence - 4 Dillon's Place - February 3, 1879

44 Spring Garden Street - March 2, 1880

3 Spring Garden Passage - December 13, 1881

40 Spring Garden Passage - October 23. 1883

Loftus Surname Ireland: 1600s to 1900s

Wedding Witnesses:

Andrew Byrne & Mary Anne Lee

- Dudley Loftus & Elizabeth Ervin – 11 May 1693 (Marriage, **St. John Parish**)

Dudley Loftus (husband):

Occupation - Doctor - May 11, 1693

Elizabeth Ervin (wife):

Occupation - Lady - May 11, 1693

- Dudley Loftus, bur. 10 Apr 1695 (Burial, **St. Patrick Parish**) & Frances Nagle, b. 1629, d. 18 Jun 1691, bur. 20 Jun 1691 (Burial, **St. Patrick Parish**)
  - Adam Loftus – bapt. 5 Nov 1654 (Baptism, **St. John Parish**), d. 10 Jul 1688, bur. 12 Jul 1688 (Burial, **St. Patrick Parish**)

Adam Loftus (son):

Age at Death - 33 years

Place of Burial - "in the burial place of his ancestors" - July 12, 1688

  - Dudley Loftus – bapt. 26 Oct 1656 (Baptism, **St. John Parish**), bur. 11 Jul 1658 (Burial, **St. John Parish**)
  - Jean Loftus – bapt. 27 Jun 1658 (Baptism, **St. John Parish**)
  - Francis Loftus – bapt. 2 Jun 1665 (Baptism, **St. John Parish**)
  - Catherine Loftus – bapt. 15 Dec 1666 (Baptism, **St. John Parish**)

Hurst

Dudley Loftus (father):

Occupation - Doctor - October 26, 1656

June 27, 1658

June 2, 1665

Esquire - December 15, 1666

Education - LL.D.

Frances Nagle, daughter of Patrick Nagle (mother):

Residence - Blind Key - June 18, 1691

Place of Burial - "among her deceased children in the burial place

of her husband's family near the altar" - June 20, 1691

- Edward Loftus & Anne Reed – 18 Mar 1758 (Marriage, **St. Mary Parish**)
  - o Elizabeth Loftus – bapt. 14 Feb 1759 (Baptism, **St. Mary Parish**)

Edward Loftus (father):

Occupation - Esquire - March 18, 1758

February 14, 1759

- Edward Loftus & Ellen Finn
  - o Gulielmo Loftus & Bridget Myers – 31 May 1860 (Marriage, **St. Catherine Parish (RC)**)

Gulielmo Loftus (son):

Residence - Vagus - May 31, 1860

Loftus Surname Ireland: 1600s to 1900s

Bridget Myers, daughter of John Myers & Ellen Pilkington (daughter-in-law):

　　Residence - Vagus - May 31, 1860

Wedding Witnesses:

John Anderson & Dora Byrne

- Edward Loftus & Mary Duffy – 8 Jan 1851 (Marriage, **Sandyford Parish (RC)**)

    o Mary Loftus – bapt. 1851 (Baptism, **Sandyford Parish (RC)**)

Wedding Witnesses:

Thomas Bohan & Catherine Connor

- Edward Loftus & Mary Loftus

    o Edward Loftus – bapt. 30 Dec 1736 (Baptism, **St. Mary Parish**)

Edward Loftus (Father):

　　Residence - Drogheda - December 30, 1736

- Edward Loftus & Mary Unknown

    o Joseph Loftus – bapt. 1842 (Baptism, **St. Andrew Parish (RC)**)

- Edward Loftus & Mary Unknown

    o Joseph Thomas Loftus – b. 8 Feb 1842, bapt. 31 Mar 1842 (Baptism, **St. Peter Parish**)

Edward Loftus (father):

　　Residence - Edinburgh - March 31, 1842

　　Occupation - Soldier - March 31, 1842

- Edward Loftus & Unknown Loftus

  - Alice Loftus – bapt. 10 Apr 1638 (Baptism, **St. Michan Parish**)

Edward Loftus (father):

Social Status - Sir, Knight

Unknown Loftus (mother):

Social Status - Dame

- George Loftus & Mary Gibbons – Unclear (Marriage, **St. James Parish**)

George Loftus (husband):

Residence - Richmond Barracks - Unclear

Occupation - He is a member of the 43rd Regiment - Unclear

- George Loftus & Unknown

  - Charlotte Loftus & David Grimmond – 10 Feb 1867 (Marriage, **St. Paul Parish**)

Signatures:

Charlotte Loftus (daughter):

Residence - 9 Montpelier Hill - February 10, 1867

Loftus Surname Ireland: 1600s to 1900s

David Grimmond, son of James Grimmond (son-in-law):

Residence - 9 Montpelier Hill - February 10, 1867

Occupation - Druggist, Chemist - February 10, 1867

James Grimmond (father):

Occupation - Engineer

George Loftus (father):

Occupation - Clerk

Wedding Witnesses:

Hugh Hillyard & Maren Hillyard

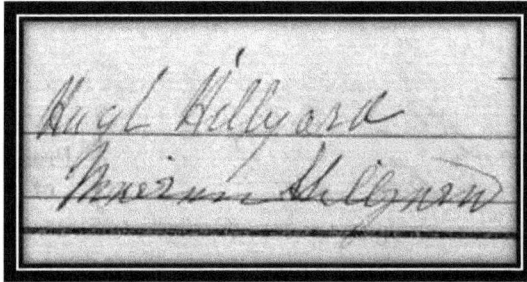

Signatures:

- Gulielmo Loftus & Mary Unknown
  - Patrick Loftus & Anne Kennedy – 5 Jul 1863 (Marriage, **St. Nicholas Parish (RC)**)
    - Patrick Loftus – b. 27 Feb 1863, bapt. 16 Mar 1863 (Baptism, **St. Nicholas Parish (RC)**)

Patrick Loftus (son):

Residence - 3 George Street - March 16, 1863

23 Chancery Lane - July 5, 1863

Hurst

Anne Kennedy, daughter of Michael Kennedy & Mary Unknown (daughter-in-law):

Residence - 23 Chancery Lane - July 5, 1863

Wedding Witnesses:

Edward Sherwood & Mary Barber

- Gulielmo Loftus & Rose Collaghan
  - Thomas Loftus – bapt. 1 Jan 1774 (Baptism, St. Nicholas Parish (RC))
  - Valentine Loftus – bapt. 1776 (Baptism, St. Andrew Parish (RC))
  - Ruth Loftus – bapt. 1779 (Baptism, St. Andrew Parish (RC))
  - Andrew Leeson Loftus – bapt. 1781 (Baptism, St. Andrew Parish (RC))
  - Eleanor Loftus – bapt. 1783 (Baptism, St. Andrew Parish (RC))
  - Gulielmo Loftus – bapt. 1785 (Baptism, St. Andrew Parish (RC))
- Henry Loftus & Frances Monroe – 14 Feb 1745 (Marriage, St. Mary Parish)

Henry Loftus (husband):

Occupation - Esquire - February 14, 1745

- Henry George Loftus & Mary Loftus
  - Henry George Loftus – b. 21 May 1860, bapt. 10 Jun 1860 (Baptism, St. George Parish)

Henry George Loftus (father):

Residence - 10 Blessington Street - June 10, 1860

Occupation - Laborer - June 10, 1860

Loftus Surname Ireland: 1600s to 1900s

- Hugh Loftus & Unknown
  - Leonard Loftus – bapt. 19 Jul 1714 (Baptism, **St. Nicholas Without Parish**), bur. 27 Dec 1714 (Burial, **St. Nicholas Without Parish**)

Leonard Loftus (son):

Residence - Patrick Street - before December 27, 1714

  - Thomas Loftus – bur. 15 Nov 1715 (Burial, **St. Nicholas Without Parish**)

Thomas Loftus (son):

Residence - Patrick Street - before November 15, 1715

Hugh Loftus (father):

Residence - Patrick Street - July 19, 1714

Occupation - Butcher - July 19, 1714

- James Loftus & Catherine Kenny
  - James Joseph Loftus – b. 29 Jan 1900, bapt. 2 Feb 1900 (Baptism, **St. Mary. Pro Cathedral Parish (RC)**)

James Loftus (father):

Residence - 25 Summer Hill - February 2, 1900

Hurst

- James Loftus & Catherine Rogers

  - Mary Catherine Loftus – b. 21 Nov 1896, bapt. 25 Nov 1896 (Baptism, **St. Mary. Pro Cathedral Parish (RC)**)

James Loftus (father):

Residence - Rotunda - November 25, 1896

- James Loftus & Catherine Unknown

  - Michael J. Loftus & Alice Kelly – 1 Feb 1903 (Marriage, **St. Mary, Haddington Road Parish (RC)**)

    - Mary Agnes Loftus – b. 29 Aug 1904, bapt. 11 Sep 1904 (Baptism, **Rathmines Parish (RC)**)

Michael J. Loftus (son):

Residence - 28 Shelburne Road - February 1, 1903

53 Mount Pleasant Square - September 11, 1904

Alice Kelly, daughter of Patrick Kelly & Alice Unknown (daughter-in-law):

Residence - 113 Haddington Road - February 1, 1903

Wedding Witnesses:

William Duncan & Luke Kelly

- James Loftus & Mary Hurly

  - Patrick Loftus – b. 7 Mar 1850, bapt. 7 Mar 1850 (Baptism, **Tralee Parish (RC)**)

Loftus Surname Ireland: 1600s to 1900s

- James Loftus & Unknown

  - Joseph John Loftus & Anne Mary Purcell – 5 Apr 1893 (Marriage, **St. James Parish (RC)**)

Joseph John Loftus (son):

Residence - Roundstone, Co. Galway - April 5, 1893

Anne Mary Purcell, daughter of John Purcell (daughter-in-law):

Residence - 8 Belton Terrace, South Circular Road - April 5, 1893

Wedding Witnesses:

C. Henry Purcell & Dalia M. Loftus

- Jervis Loftus & Hetcher Loftus

  - Harry Loftus – bapt. 13 Mar 1736 (Baptism, **St. Mary Parish**)

- John Loftus & Alice Unknown, b. 1837, d. 19 Jan 1894, bur. 1894 (Burial, **Clondalkin Parish**)

  - Frances Loftus – b. 1864, bapt. 1864 (Baptism, **Clondalkin Parish**)

  - Mary Anne Loftus – b. 1866, bapt. 1866 (Baptism, **Clondalkin Parish**)

  - William Loftus – b. 1868, bapt. 1868 (Baptism, **Clondalkin Parish**), d. 20 Nov 1876, bur. 1876 (Burial, **Clondalkin Parish**)

William Loftus (son):

Residence - Baldonnell, Clondalkin - November 20, 1876

Age at Death - 8 years

  - Edward Loftus – b. 1871, bapt. 1871 (Baptism, **Clondalkin Parish**)

  - Benjamin Loftus – b. 1874, bapt. 1874 (Baptism, **Clondalkin Parish**)

John Loftus (father):

Hurst

Residence - BalDonnell, Clondalkin - 1864

Naas Road, Clondalkin - 1866

Corkagh - 1868

BalDonnell - 1871

1874

Occupation - Laborer - 1864

1866

1868

Gardiner - 1874

Alice Unknown (mother):

Residence - Tipperary - January 19, 1894

Age at Death - 57 years

- John Loftus & Anne Delany – 10 Aug 1837 (Marriage, **St. Andrew Parish (RC)**)

  o Bridget Anne Loftus – bapt. 26 Dec 1838 (Baptism, **St. Catherine Parish (RC)**)

  o John Loftus – bapt. 22 Nov 1840 (Baptism, **St. Catherine Parish (RC)**)

  o Patrick Loftus – bapt. 5 Feb 1843 (Baptism, **St. Catherine Parish (RC)**)

  o Mary Loftus – bapt. 30 Mar 1845 (Baptism, **St. Catherine Parish (RC)**)

  o Patrick Loftus – bapt. 30 Jun 1848 (Baptism, **St. Catherine Parish (RC)**)

  o Jane Loftus – b. 14 Apr 1858, bapt. 20 Apr 1858 (Baptism, **St. Catherine Parish (RC)**)

  o Anne Jane Loftus – b. 24 Jan 1860, bapt. 27 Jan 1860 (Baptism, **St. Catherine Parish (RC)**)

Loftus Surname Ireland: 1600s to 1900s

John Loftus (father):

Residence - 16 Thomas Street - April 20, 1858

35 New Row - January 27, 1860

Wedding Witnesses:

James Fagan & Mary Anne Mulholland

- John Loftus & Anne Unknown
  - Bridget Loftus & Joseph Brown – 19 Aug 1866 (Marriage, **St. Nicholas Parish (RC)**)
    - John Joseph Brown – b. 20 Aug 1868, bapt. 20 Aug 1868 (Baptism, **St. Audoen Parish (RC)**)
    - Mary Josephine Brown – b. 2 Jun 1870, bapt. 3 Jun 1870 (Baptism, **St. Audoen Parish (RC)**)
    - Christopher Michael Brown – b. 5 Jan 1873, bapt. 9 Jan 1873 (Baptism, **SS. Michael & John Parish (RC)**)
    - Bridget Anne Brown – b. 28 Apr 1875, bapt. 4 May 1875 (Baptism, **St. Audoen Parish (RC)**)
    - Josephina Brown – b. 15 Mar 1878, bapt. 15 Mar 1878 (Baptism, **St. Nicholas Parish (RC)**)
    - Margaret Mary Brown – b. 15 Mar 1878, bapt. 15 Mar 1878 (Baptism, **St. Nicholas Parish (RC)**)

Bridget Loftus (daughter):

Residence - 5 Lamb Alley - August 19, 1866

Hurst

Joseph Brown, son of Michael Brown & Bridget Unknown (son-in-law):

Residence - 45 High Street - August 19, 1866

No. 1 Corn Market - August 20, 1868

6 Corn Market - June 3, 1870

44 High Street - January 9, 1873

May 4, 1875

3 Lamb Alley - March 15, 1878

Wedding Witnesses:

Thomas Nolan & Sarah F. Avoy

- John Loftus & Catherine Field – 20 Mar 1768 or 20 Mar 1769 (Marriage, St. Catherine Parish (RC))

Wedding Witnesses:

John Broderick & John Bridget Lacey

- John Loftus & Catherine Maher
  - Mary Anne Loftus – bapt. 11 Nov 1770 (Baptism, St. Catherine Parish (RC))
- John Loftus & Catherine McHilland – 13 Feb 1832 (Marriage, St. Peter Parish)

John Loftus (husband):

Residence - Stephen's Green, St. Peter Parish - February 13, 1832

Catherine McHilland (wife):

Residence - Stephen's Green - February 13, 1832

Loftus Surname Ireland: 1600s to 1900s

Wedding Witnesses:

Charles Wilson & Thomas Ritchie

- John Loftus & Catherine Unknown

    - John Loftus & Bridget McDonnell – 1 Nov 1863 (Marriage, **St. Nicholas Parish (RC)**)

        - John Loftus – b. 27 Aug 1864, bapt. 2 Sep 1864 (Baptism, **St. Nicholas Parish (RC)**)

        - Christine Loftus – b. 5 Jan 1879, bapt. 2 Feb 1879 (Baptism, **St. Nicholas Parish (RC)**)

John Loftus (son):

Residence - 9 Lower Camden Street - November 1, 1863

September 2, 1864

38 Bishop Street - February 2, 1879

Bridget McDonnell, daughter of Matthew McDonnell & Anne Unknown

(daughter-in-law):

Residence - 9 Lower Camden Street - November 1, 1863

Wedding Witnesses:

Christopher Fitzgerald & Louisa Fay

- John Loftus & Easter Sharp – 29 Jul 1698 (Marriage, **St. Catherine Parish**)

    - Mary Loftus – bapt. 6 Jan 1705 (Baptism, **St. Catherine Parish**)

- John Loftus & Elizabeth Loftus

    - Gulielmo Loftus & Teresa Keefe – 20 Mar 1857 (Marriage, **St. Mary. Pro Cathedral Parish (RC)**)

Hurst

Gulielmo Loftus (son):

Residence - 10 Summer Hill - March 20, 1857

Teresa Keefe, daughter of Patrick Keefe & Alice Keefe (daughter-in-law):

Residence - 5 Ryder's Row - March 20, 1857

Wedding Witnesses:

Hugh O'Reilly & James Kerwick

- John Loftus & Emily Fay
  - Catherine Mary Loftus – b. 23 Sep 1886, bapt. 4 Oct 1886 (Baptism, **St. Mary. Pro Cathedral Parish** (RC))

John Loftus (father):

Residence - 35 North Gloucester Place - October 4, 1886

- John Loftus & Henrietta Unknown
  - Richard Valentine Loftus – b. 1880, bapt. 1880 (Baptism, **Lucan Parish**)

John Loftus (father):

Residence - Lucan - 1880

Occupation - Coachman - 1880

- John Loftus & Jane Unknown, bur. 5 Sep 1673 (Burial, **St. Michan Parish**)

John Loftus (husband):

Occupation - Sergeant of Foot [Regiment] - September 5, 1673

Loftus Surname Ireland: 1600s to 1900s

- John Loftus & Julia Keegan

  - Jane Loftus – b. 1866, bapt. 1866 (Baptism, **St. Andrew Parish** (RC))

John Loftus (father):

Residence - 11 Misery Hill - 1866

- John Loftus & Margaret Maxwell

  - Patrick Loftus – bapt. 11 Mar 1835 (Baptism, **St. Nicholas Parish** (RC))

  - Margaret Loftus – bapt. 23 Sep 1836 (Baptism, **St. Nicholas Parish** (RC))

  - Luke Loftus – bapt. 3 Dec 1841 (Baptism, **St. Nicholas Parish** (RC))

  - John Loftus – bapt. 27 Oct 1845 (Baptism, **St. Nicholas Parish** (RC))

- John Loftus & Margaret Unknown

  - Michael Loftus – bapt. 28 Feb 1804 (Baptism, **St. James Parish** (RC))

- John Loftus & Margaret Unknown

  - Susan Loftus & Peter Branagan – 1 Jul 1860 (Marriage, **St. Nicholas Parish** (RC))

Susan Loftus (daughter):

Residence - 9 Hanover Lane - July 1, 1860

Peter Branagan, son of Thomas Branagan & Margaret Unknown (son-in-law):

Residence - 25 East Essex Street - July 1, 1860

Wedding Witnesses:

Francis Short & Bridget Short

Hurst

- John Loftus & Mary Harrison – 14 Aug 1863 (Marriage, **St. Catherine Parish** (RC))

  o Margaret Loftus – b. 6 Jul 1867, bapt. 15 Jul 1867 (Baptism, **St. Nicholas Parish** (RC))

  o Michael Loftus – b. 2 Oct 1869, bapt. 15 Oct 1869 (Baptism, **St. Nicholas Parish** (RC))

  o Mary Susan Loftus – b. 22 Jan 1872, bapt. 5 Feb 1872 (Baptism, **St. Nicholas Parish** (RC))

  o John Joseph Loftus – b. 5 Jul 1875, bapt. 16 Jul 1875 (Baptism, **St. Nicholas Parish** (RC))

  o Mary Ellen Loftus – b. 17 Jul 1877, bapt. 23 Jul 1877 (Baptism, **St. Nicholas Parish** (RC))

John Loftus (father):

Residence - 3 Patrick Close - July 15, 1867

4 Plunket Street - October 15, 1869

July 16, 1875

1 Great Ship Street - January 22, 1872

6 Plunket Street - July 23, 1877

Wedding Witnesses:

Charles McGuigan & Anne Morris

- John Loftus & Mary Loftus

  o John Loftus – bapt. 10 Feb 1837 (Baptism, **St. Mary. Pro Cathedral Parish** (RC))

- John Loftus & Mary Loftus

  o Anne Loftus – b. 15 Apr 1854, bapt. 14 May 1854 (Baptism, **Aghold Parish**)

  o Elizabeth Loftus, bapt. 18 Jul 1856 (Baptism, **Aghold Parish**) & Robert Bridges – 31 Mar 1886 (Marriage, **Aghold Parish**)

Loftus Surname Ireland: 1600s to 1900s

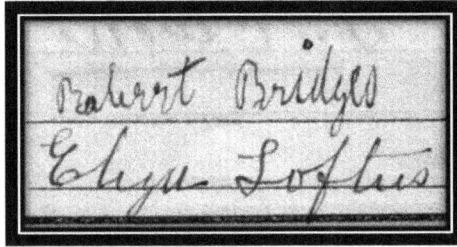

Signatures:

Elizabeth Loftus (daughter):

    Residence - Knockloe - March 31, 1886

Robert Bridges, son of Robert Bridges (son-in-law):

    Residence - Knockloe - March 31, 1886

    Occupation - Servant - March 31, 1886

Robert Bridges (father):

    Occupation - Farmer

John Loftus (father):

    Occupation - Farmer

Wedding Witnesses:

Richard Loftus & Elizabeth Loftus

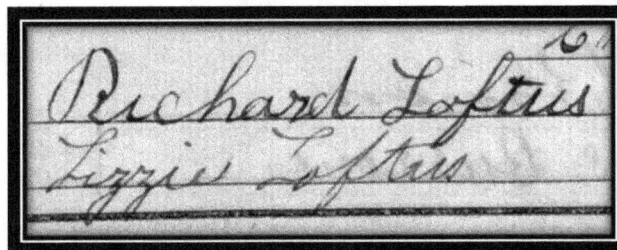

Signatures:

Hurst

- William Loftus – b. 4 Dec 1859, bapt. 8 Jan 1860 (Baptism, **Aghold Parish**)
- Thomas Loftus – b. 14 Mar 1862, bapt. 24 Mar 1862 (Baptism, **Aghold Parish**), bur. 29 Mar 1862 (Burial, **Aghold Parish**)

Thomas Loftus (son):

Residence - Rath - before March 29, 1862

Age at Death - 15 days

- Thomas Loftus – b. 5 Jun 1863, bapt. 12 Jul 1863 (Baptism, **Aghold Parish**)
- Valentine Loftus – b. 13 Oct 1866, bapt. 9 Dec 1866 (Baptism, **Aghold Parish**)
- Richard Loftus – b. 7 Dec 1867, bapt. 9 Feb 1868 (Baptism, **Aghold Parish**)
- John Loftus – b. 27 Nov 1869, bapt. 15 Dec 1869 (Baptism, **Aghold Parish**)
- Alice Loftus – b. 26 Dec 1872, bapt. 31 Dec 1872 (Baptism, **Aghold Parish**), bur. 2 Jan 1873 (Burial, **Aghold Parish**)

Alice Loftus (daughter):

Residence - Knocklow - before January 2, 1873

Age at Death - 1 week

John Loftus (father):

Residence - Knocklow - May 14, 1854

July 18, 1856

January 8, 1860

December 31, 1872

Loftus Surname Ireland: 1600s to 1900s

Rath - March 24, 1862

July 12, 1863

December 9, 1866

February 9, 1868

December 15, 1869

Occupation - Laborer - May 14, 1854

July 18, 1856

December 15, 1869

December 31, 1872

Farmer - January 8, 1860

December 9, 1866

February 9, 1868

Servant - March 24, 1862

July 12, 1863

- John Loftus & Mary Unknown
  - Frances Loftus – bapt. 27 Sep 1783 (Baptism, **St. Nicholas Parish (RC)**)
- John Loftus & Rose Donohoe
  - Mary Loftus – b. 1869, bapt. 1869 (Baptism, **St. Andrew Parish (RC)**)

John Loftus (father):

Residence - 11 Hanover Street - 1869

Hurst

- John Loftus & Unknown

  - o Joseph Loftus & Bridget Flemming – 6 Dec 1858 (Marriage, **St. Peter Parish**)

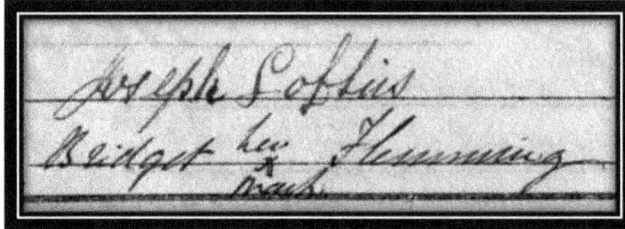

Signatures:

Joseph Loftus (son):

    Residence - Portobello Barracks - December 6, 1858

    Occupation - Gunner, Royal Artillery - December 6, 1858

Bridget Flemming, daughter of Thomas Flemming (daughter-in-law):

    Residence - 1 Toole's Cottages - December 6, 1858

Thomas Flemming (father):

    Occupation - Carpenter

John Loftus (father):

    Occupation - Farmer

Wedding Witnesses:

Richard Irwin & Mary Everard

Loftus Surname Ireland: 1600s to 1900s

Signatures:

- John Loftus & Unknown

  o John Loftus & Mary McLoughlin – 9 May 1882 (Marriage, **St. Andrew Parish** (RC))

    ▪ John Loftus – b. 1882, bapt. 1882 (Baptism, **St. Andrew Parish** (RC))

    ▪ Joseph Patrick Loftus – b. 1885, bapt. 1885 (Baptism, **St. Andrew Parish** (RC))

    ▪ Joseph Loftus – b. 1892, bapt. 1892 (Baptism, **St. Andrew Parish** (RC))

    ▪ Margaret Loftus – b. 1894, bapt. 1894 (Baptism, **St. Andrew Parish** (RC))

    ▪ Peter Loftus – b. 1899, bapt. 1899 (Baptism, **St. Andrew Parish** (RC))

    ▪ James Loftus – b. 1901, bapt. 1901 (Baptism, **St. Andrew Parish** (RC))

John Loftus (son):

Residence - 11 Brunswick Street - May 9, 1882

11 Brunswick Place - 1882

2 Sandwith Place - 1885

15 Lower Erne Street - 1892

1 Peterson's Lane - 1894

1899

1901

Hurst

Margaret McLoughlin, daughter of Joseph McLoughlin (daughter-in-law):

Residence - 11 Brunswick Street - May 9, 1882

Wedding Witnesses:

Joseph McLoughlin & Margaret Kelly

- John Loftus & Unknown
  - Mary Anne Loftus & William Scully – 20 Mar 1900 (Marriage, St. Matthias Parish)

Signatures:

Mary Anne Loftus (daughter):

Residence - 7 Adelaide Road, Dublin - March 20, 1900

William Scully, son of Francis Scully (son-in-law):

Residence - Birch Grove, Roserea - March 20, 1900

Occupation - Coachman - March 20, 1900

Francis Scully (father):

Occupation - Laborer

John Loftus (father):

Residence - Gardener

Loftus Surname Ireland: 1600s to 1900s

Wedding Witnesses:

Jane Scully & Edward Loftus

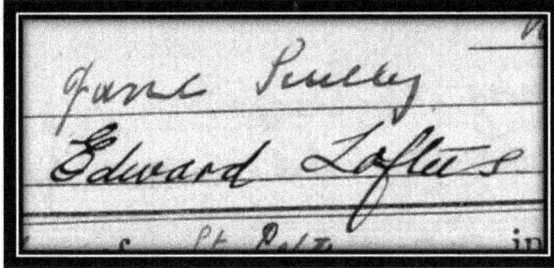

Signatures:

- John Loftus & Winifred Unknown

    o John Loftus – bapt. 1832 (Baptism, **St. Andrew Parish (RC)**)

- Jonathan Loftus & Judith Unknown

    o Esther Loftus – bapt. 1 Apr 1743 (Baptism, **St. Michan Parish (RC)**)

    o John Loftus – bapt. 31 Mar 1745 (Baptism, **St. Michan Parish (RC)**)

    o Mary Loftus – bapt. 23 Dec 1750 (Baptism, **St. Michan Parish (RC)**)

Jonathan Loftus (father):

Residence - Ormond Quay - April 1, 1743

Hurst

- Lord Adam Loftus & Unknown

  o Marian Loftus & Robert O'Brien Studdert – 12 Feb 1874 (Marriage, **St. Anne Parish**)

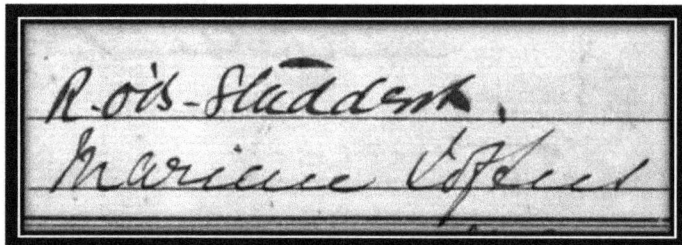

Signatures:

Marian Loftus (daughter):

    Residence - Belvoir, Co. Clare - February 12, 1874

Robert O'Brien Studdert, son of Robert Wogan Studdert (son-in-law):

    Residence - 14 Dawson Street - February 12, 1874

    Occupation - Esquire - February 12, 1874

Robert Wogan Studdert (father):

    Occupation - Esquire

Lord Adam Loftus (father):

    Occupation - Clerk in Holy Orders

Wedding Witnesses:

Henry Loftus, M. Loftus, & G. Loftus

Loftus Surname Ireland: 1600s to 1900s

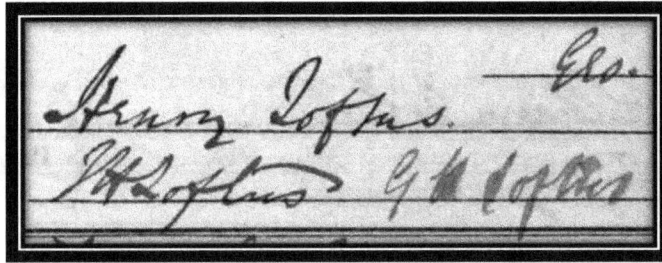

Signatures:

- Leeson Loftus & Elizabeth Loftus

    o William Loftus – b. 9 Oct 1691 (Baptism, **St. Michan Parish**), bur. 26 Oct 1691 (Burial, **St. Michan Parish**)

Leeson Loftus (father):

Occupation - Gentleman - October 9, 1691

October 26, 1691

- Luke Loftus & Bridget McGail

    o Thomas Loftus & Elizabeth Donnelly – 23 May 1900 (Marriage, **St. Mary, Donnybrook Parish (RC)**)

Thomas Loftus (son):

Residence - 7 Dodd's Cottages, Terenure - May 23, 1900

Elizabeth Donnelly, daughter of William Donnelly & Margaret Nolan

(daughter-in-law):

Residence - 37 Morehampton Terrace - May 23, 1900

Wedding Witnesses:

Michael Hoskins & Catherine Keogh

Hurst

- Luke Loftus & Unknown

  o Mary Loftus & Thomas Stroud – 29 Nov 1881 (Marriage, **Kilmainham Parish**)

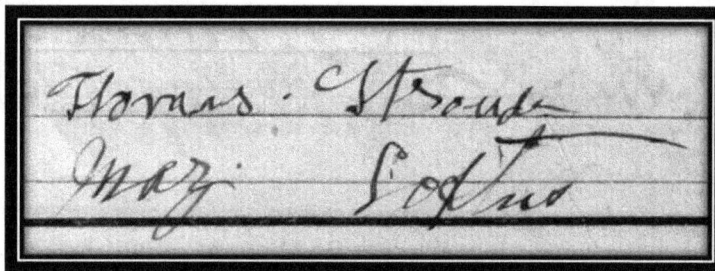

Signatures:

Mary Loftus (daughter):

Residence - 6 Albion Terrace, Golden Bridge - November 29, 1881

Thomas Stroud, son of William Stroud (son-in-law):

Residence - Island Bridge Barracks - November 29, 1881

Occupation - Private, 1st Royal Dragoons - November 29, 1881

William Stroud (father):

Occupation - Bricklayer

Luke Loftus (father):

Occupation - Servant

Wedding Witnesses:

William Clayton & Lucy Raden

Loftus Surname Ireland: 1600s to 1900s

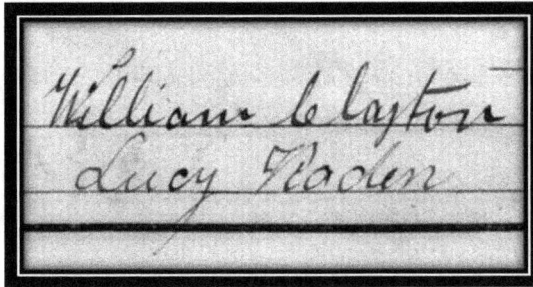

Signatures:

- Martin Loftus & Esther Unknown

    o Mary Loftus – bapt. 25 Jun 1843 (Baptism, **St. Mary. Pro Cathedral Parish (RC)**)

    o Michael Loftus – bapt. 10 Aug 1845 (Baptism, **St. Mary. Pro Cathedral Parish (RC)**)

    o Teresa Loftus – bapt. 14 Jan 1849 (Baptism, **St. Mary. Pro Cathedral Parish (RC)**)

- Martin Loftus & Susan Lawler

    o George Loftus – bapt. Feb 1833 (Baptism, **St. Catherine Parish (RC)**)

- Martin Loftus & Susan Unknown

    o Thomas Loftus – bapt. 6 Aug 1822 (Baptism, **St. Mary. Pro Cathedral Parish (RC)**)

Martin Loftus (father):

Residence - Summer Hill - August 6, 1822

- Matthew Loftus & Margaret Dooling – 25 Nov 1805 (Marriage, **St. Mary. Pro Cathedral Parish (RC)**)

Wedding Witnesses:

Dennis Flinn & Mary Dooling

Hurst

- Matthew John Loftus & Unknown

  o Mary Josephine Loftus & William Henry Robert De Molines – 30 Jun 1870 (Marriage, St. Peter Parish)

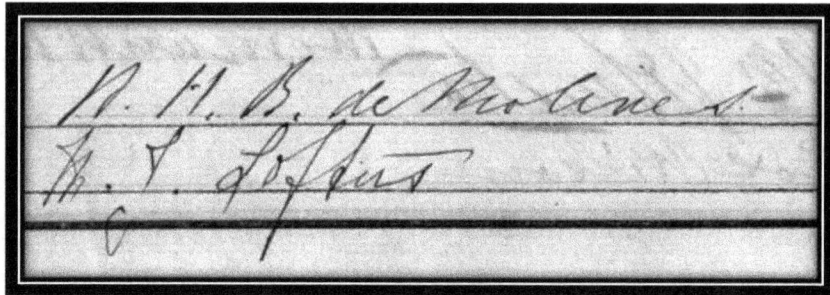

Signatures:

Mary Josephine Loftus (daughter):

Residence - 101 Lower Baggot Street - June 30, 1870

William Henry Robert De Molines, son of William De Molines (son-in-law):

Residence - 100 Lower Baggot Street - June 30, 1870

Occupation - Barrister at Law - June 30, 1870

William De Molines (father):

Occupation - Esquire

Matthew John Loftus (father):

Occupation - Esquire

Wedding Witnesses:

W. J. Loftus & T. Marion Loftus

Loftus Surname Ireland: 1600s to 1900s

Signatures:

- Michael Loftus & Alice McCreely

  o Mary Anne Loftus – bapt. Jan 1852 (Baptism, **St. Michan Parish (RC)**)

- Michael Loftus & Bridget Heavy

  o Margaret Loftus – b. 15 Jul 1855, bapt. 8 Aug 1855 (Baptism, **St. Mary. Pro Cathedral Parish (RC)**)

  o Michael Joseph Loftus – b. 27 Jun 1860, bapt. 6 Jul 1860 (Baptism, **St. Mary. Pro Cathedral Parish (RC)**)

Michael Loftus (father):

Residence - 7 Hutton's Lane - August 8, 1855

36 Mount Joy Square Street - July 6, 1860

- Michael Loftus & Bridget Unknown

  o Olivia Loftus – bapt. Jul 1851 (Baptism, **SS. Michael & John Parish (RC)**)

- Michael Loftus & Elizabeth Walsh

  o John Joseph Loftus – b. 25 Mar 1892, bapt. 31 Mar 1892 (Baptism, **SS. Michael & John Parish (RC)**)

  o Michael Loftus – b. 9 Aug 1896, bapt. 10 Aug 1896 (Baptism, **SS. Michael & John Parish (RC)**)

Hurst

Michael Loftus (father):

Residence - 2 Longford Lane - March 31, 1892

52 Stephen Street - August 10, 1896

- Michael Loftus & Mary Kelly
  - Michael Joseph Loftus – b. 19 Nov 1905, bapt. 6 Dec 1905 (Baptism, **Rathmines Parish (RC)**)

Michael Loftus (father):

Residence - 8 Richmond Place - December 6, 1905

- Michael Loftus & Susan Casey
  - Anne Loftus – bapt. 3 Sep 1850 (Baptism, **St. Catherine Parish** (RC))
- Michael Loftus & Susan Unknown
  - Margaret Loftus & Thomas Mahon – 15 Nov 1857 (Marriage, **St. Catherine Parish** (RC))

Margaret Loftus (daughter):

Residence - 34 Meath Street - November 15, 1857

Thomas Mahon, son of Thomas Mahon & Bridget Unknown (son-in-law):

Residence - Linen Hall Barracks - November 15, 1857

Wedding Witnesses:

Thomas Loftus & Bridget Bedney

Loftus Surname Ireland: 1600s to 1900s

- Nicholas Loftus & Anne Loftus

  o Henry Loftus – b. 18 Nov 1709, bapt. 28 Nov 1709 (Baptism, **St. Mary Parish**)

  o John Ponsonby Loftus – b. 10 Mar 1714, bapt. 9 Apr 1714 (Baptism, **St. Mary Parish**), bur. 26 Apr 1714 (Burial, **St. Mary Parish**)

Nicholas Loftus (father):

Occupation - Esquire - November 28, 1709

April 9, 1714

- Nicholas Loftus & Mary Loftus

  o Mary Loftus – bapt. 22 Apr 1710 (Baptism, **St. Paul Parish**)

- Nicholas Loftus & Susanna Alderly – 26 Feb 1662 (Marriage, **St. Michan Parish**)

Nicholas Loftus (husband):

Social Status - Sir, Knight

- Patrick Loftus & Anne Byrne (B y r n e)

  o David Loftus – b. 11 Oct 1881, bapt. 14 Oct 1881 (Baptism, **St. Mary. Pro Cathedral Parish (RC)**)

  o Christine Bridget Loftus – b. 23 Dec 1885, bapt. 28 Dec 1885 (Baptism, **St. Mary. Pro Cathedral Parish (RC)**)

Patrick Loftus (father):

Residence - 24 Lower Mecklenburgh Street - October 14, 1881

December 28, 1885

Hurst

- Patrick Loftus & Anne Unknown

  - Thomas Loftus & Catherine Coghlan – 1 Aug 1870 (Marriage, **St. Nicholas Parish (RC)**)

Thomas Loftus (son):

Residence - 16 Chancery Lane - August 1, 1870

Catherine Coghlan, daughter of John Coghlan & Catherine Hayes

(daughter-in-law):

Residence - 27 Bride Street - August 1, 1870

Wedding Witnesses:

Mary Kennedy & Bridget Rigney

- Patrick Loftus & Margaret Loftus

  - Michael Loftus – bapt. 23 Sep 1826 (Baptism, **St. Mary. Pro Cathedral Parish (RC)**)

  - Margaret Harriet Loftus – bapt. 8 Apr 1828 (Baptism, **St. Mary. Pro Cathedral Parish (RC)**)

  - Patrick Loftus – bapt. 13 Apr 1830 (Baptism, **St. Mary. Pro Cathedral Parish (RC)**)

  - Margaret Loftus – bapt. 6 May 1833 (Baptism, **St. Mary. Pro Cathedral Parish (RC)**)

Patrick Loftus (father):

Residence - Blessington Street - September 23, 1826

Britain Street - April 8, 1828

Loftus Surname Ireland: 1600s to 1900s

- Patrick Loftus & Margaret Loftus
  - Bridget Loftus & Abraham Sherry – 26 Jul 1864 (Marriage, **St. Mary. Pro Cathedral Parish (RC)**)
    - Mary Margaret Sherry, b. 7 Aug 1862, bapt. 27 Aug 1862 (Baptism, **St. Mary. Pro Cathedral Parish (RC)**) & Thomas Byrne (B y r n e) – 19 Aug 1900 (Marriage, **St. Mary. Pro Cathedral Parish (RC)**)

Mary Margaret Sherry (daughter):

Residence - *5* Denmark Row - August 19, 1900

Thomas Byrne, son of Patrick Byrne & Lucy Gore (son-in-law):

Residence - 12 Riddal's Row - August 19, 1900

Wedding Witnesses:

Patrick Dolan & Catherine Cullen

- John Sherry – b. 6 May 1865, bapt. 17 May 1865 (Baptism, **St. Mary. Pro Cathedral Parish (RC)**)

- Bridget Sherry – b. 17 May 1867, bapt. 31 May 1867 (Baptism, **St. Mary. Pro Cathedral Parish (RC)**)

- Emily Mary Sherry – b. 21 Apr 1870, bapt. 25 May 1870 (Baptism, **St. Mary. Pro Cathedral Parish (RC)**)

- Ellen Sherry – bapt. 4 Oct 1872, bapt. 16 Oct 1872 (Baptism, **St. Michan Parish (RC)**)

Bridget Loftus (daughter):

Residence - 22 Mary's Abbey - July 26, 1864

Hurst

Abraham Sherry, son of Thomas Sherry & Bridget Sherry (son-in-law):

Residence - 27 Abbey Street - August 27, 1862

May 17, 1865

133 Upper Abbey Street - July 26, 1864

21 Upper Abbey Street - May 31, 1867

6 Britain Street - May 25, 1870

28 Fisher's Lane - October 16, 1872

Wedding Witnesses:

Patrick Kerwick & Isabella Hawkins

- Patrick Loftus & Margaret Unknown
  - Margaret Loftus & William Kearns (K e a r n s) – 26 Oct 1863 (Marriage, **St. Nicholas Parish** (RC))
    - Margaret Kearns (K e a r n s) – b. 1 Mar 1865, bapt. 13 Mar 1865 (Baptism, **St. Nicholas Parish** (RC))
    - Margaret Kearns (K e a r n s) – b. 22 Jun 1867, bapt. 1 Jul 1867 (Baptism, **St. Nicholas Parish** (RC))
    - John Kearns (K e a r n s) – b. 1 May 1870, bapt. 9 May 1870 (Baptism, **St. Nicholas Parish** (RC))
    - Margaret Kearns (K e a r n s) & John Smyth – 19 Nov 1899 (Marriage, **Harrington Street Parish** (RC))

Loftus Surname Ireland: 1600s to 1900s

Margaret Kearns (daughter):

    Residence - 9 Harcourt Terrace - November 19, 1899

John Smyth, son of James Smyth & Margaret McKellys (son-in-law):

    Residence - 1 Queen's Square - November 19, 1899

Wedding Witnesses:

Charles Smyth & Mary O'Callaghan

Margaret Loftus (daughter):

    Residence - 7 Bishop Place - October 26, 1863

William Kearns, son of Charles Kearns & Catherine Unknown (son-in-law):

    Residence - 123 Francis Street - October 26, 1863

        20 Plunket Street - March 13, 1865

        8 Plunket Street - July 1, 1867

        7 Bishop Court - May 9, 1870

Wedding Witnesses:

Mary Morris & Margaret Loftus

- Patrick Loftus & Margaret Wilson
  - Patrick Loftus – bapt. 27 Jul 1849 (Baptism, **St. Catherine Parish (RC)**)
- Patrick Loftus & Mary Loftus
  - Charles Loftus – bapt. 14 Jul 1826 (Baptism, **St. Mary. Pro Cathedral Parish (RC)**)
  - James Loftus – bapt. 24 Jan 1828 (Baptism, **St. Mary. Pro Cathedral Parish (RC)**)

Hurst

Patrick Loftus (father):

Residence - Temple Court - July 14, 1826

Gardner Street - January 24, 1828

- Patrick Loftus & Mary Unknown
  - Patrick Loftus – bapt. 31 Oct 1823 (Baptism, **St. Mary. Pro Cathedral Parish (RC)**)

Patrick Loftus (father):

Residence - Stephen's Green - October 31, 1823

- Peter Loftus & Elizabeth Unknown
  - Patrick Loftus – bapt. 26 Sep 1754 (Baptism, **St. James Parish (RC)**)
- Peter Loftus & Mary Cronin
  - Elizabeth Loftus – b. 30 Jun 1850, bapt. 30 Jun 1850 (Baptism, **Killarney Parish (RC)**)

Peter Loftus (father):

Residence - Killarney - June 30, 1850

- Richard Loftus & Annette Loftus
  - Mary Anne Loftus – b. 12 Jun 1898, bapt. 31 Jul 1898 (Baptism, **Aghold Parish**)
  - Alice Evelyn Loftus – b. 22 Jul 1899, bapt. 10 Sep 1899 (Baptism, **Aghold Parish**)
  - Thomas Henry Loftus – b. 8 Aug 1900, bapt. 14 Oct 1900 (Baptism, **Aghold Parish**)

Richard Loftus (father):

Residence - Nickeen - July 31, 1898

Knockeen - September 10, 1899

October 14, 1900

Occupation - Farmer - July 31, 1898

September 10, 1899

October 14, 1900

- Richard Loftus & Bridget Unknown
  - ○ Olivia Loftus & James O'Connor – 2 May 1877 (Marriage, **St. Mary. Pro Cathedral Parish (RC)**)
    - ▪ James Joseph O'Connor – b. 19 Jun 1887, bapt. 1 Jul 1887 (Baptism, **St. Mary. Pro Cathedral Parish (RC)**)

Olivia Loftus (daughter):

Residence - 13 Upper Buckingham Street - May 2, 1877

James O'Connor, son of Bryan O'Connor & Catherine O'Connor (son-in-law):

Residence - Ballybough - May 2, 1877

9 Summer Hill Place - July 1, 1887

Wedding Witnesses:

Gulielmo Kerwick & Elizabeth Shorton

- Richard Loftus & Elizabeth Cooper, b. 1819 (1st Marriage)
  - ○ Alice Loftus – bapt. 14 Dec 1845 (Baptism, **Aghold Parish**)
  - ○ Alice Loftus – b. 26 Nov 1851, bapt. 18 Jul 1856 (Baptism, **Aghold Parish**)
  - ○ Catherine Loftus – b. 29 Apr 1854, bapt. 18 Jul 1856 (Baptism, **Aghold Parish**)

Hurst

Richard Loftus (father):

Residence - Knockeen - December 14, 1845

July 18, 1856

Occupation - Farmer - December 14, 1845

July 18, 1856

Laborer - July 18, 1856

Elizabeth Cooper, daughter of Simon Cooper.

- Elizabeth Cooper Loftus (2nd Marriage), b. 1819 & Thomas Kavanagh, b. 1809 – 23 May 1859 (Marriage, **Aghold Parish**)

Signatures:

Loftus Surname Ireland: 1600s to 1900s

Elizabeth Cooper Loftus (wife):

    Residence - Nickeen, Aghold Parish - May 23, 1859

    Relationship Status at Marriage - widow

Thomas Kavanagh (husband):

    Residence - Munny, Aghold Parish - May 23, 1859

    Occupation - Steward - May 23, 1859

    Relationship Status at Marriage - widow

Simon Cooper (father):

    Occupation - Farmer

Wedding Witnesses:

William Cooper & John James

Signatures:

- Richard Loftus & Elizabeth Shean – 17 Mar 1836 (Marriage, **Aghold Parish**)

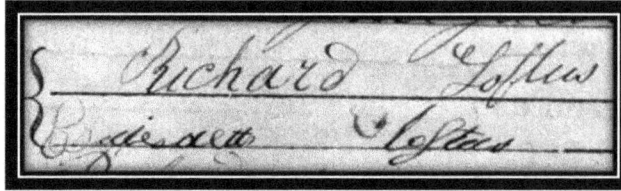

Signatures:

Richard Loftus (husband):

    Residence - Liscolman Parish - March 17, 1836

Elizabeth Sheane (wife):

    Residence - Aghold Parish - March 17, 1836

Wedding Witnesses:

Richard Shean & John Shean

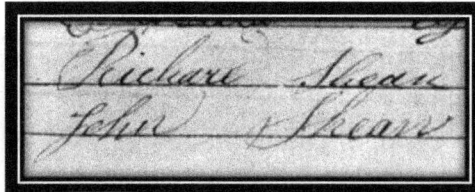

Signatures:

- Richard Loftus & Mary Codd

  - Anne Mary Loftus, b. 1846, bapt. 1870 (Baptism, **St. Andrew Parish (RC)**) & John Molloy

    – 7 Feb 1870 (Marriage, **St. Andrew Parish (RC)**)

    - Mary Anne Molloy – b. 1870, bapt. 1870 (Baptism, **St. Andrew Parish (RC)**)

Anne Mary Loftus (daughter):

    Residence - 4 Cumberland Street - February 7, 1870

Loftus Surname Ireland: 1600s to 1900s

John Molloy, son of Nicholas Molloy (son-in-law):

Residence - 2 Merrion Square - February 7, 1870

Cumberland Street - 1870

Wedding Witnesses:

Patrick J. Ryan & Bridget Kilkenny

Richard Loftus (father):

Residence - 4 Cumberland Street - 1870

- Richard Loftus & Mary Loftus
  - Richard Loftus, bapt. 9 Apr 1837 (Baptism, **Aghold Parish**) & Mary Anne Codd – 1 Dec 1859 (Marriage, **Aghold Parish**)

Signatures:

Hurst

- Margaret Loftus, b. 28 Sep 1860, bapt. 11 Nov 1860 (Baptism, **Aghold Parish**) & John Rose – 31 Dec 1885 (Marriage, **Aghold Parish**)

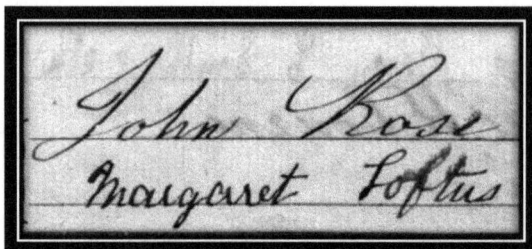

Signatures:

Margaret Loftus (daughter):

    Residence - Rath - December 31, 1885

    Occupation - Farmer - December 31, 1885

John Rose, son of James Rose (son-in-law):

    Residence - Coonogue, Co. Carlow - December 31, 1885

    Occupation - Farmer - December 31, 1885

James Rose (father):

    Occupation - Farmer

Richard Loftus (father):

    Occupation - Farmer

Wedding Witnesses:

William Rigley & Matthew Codd

Loftus Surname Ireland: 1600s to 1900s

Signatures:

- Elizabeth Loftus, b. 29 Sep 1862, bapt. 14 Dec 1862 (Baptism, **Aghold Parish**) & Thomas

  Hopkins – 30 Oct 1895 (Marriage, **Aghold Parish**)

Signatures:

Elizabeth Loftus (daughter):

    Residence - Knockeen - October 30, 1895

    Occupation - Farmer - October 30. 1895

Thomas Hopkins, son of Robert Hopkins (son-in-law):

    Residence - Moyne - October 30, 1895

    Occupation - Farmer - October 30, 1895

Robert Hopkins (father):

    Occupation - Farmer

Richard Loftus (father):

    Occupation - Farmer

Hurst

Wedding Witnesses:

Robert Bryan & Mary Anne Loftus

Signatures:

- Mary Anne Loftus, b. 6 Mar 1865, bapt. 9 Mar 1865 (Baptism, **Aghold Parish**) & Joseph

   Robert – 11 Jun 1896 (Marriage, **Aghold Parish**)

Signature:

Signatures (Marriage):

Mary Anne Loftus (daughter):

   Residence - Knockeen - June 11, 1896

   Occupation - Farmer - June 11, 1896

Loftus Surname Ireland: 1600s to 1900s

Joseph Roberts, son of Joshua Roberts (son-in-law):

Residence - Barushusk - June 11, 1896

Occupation - Farmer - June 11, 1896

Joshua Roberts (father):

Occupation - Farmer

Richard Loftus (father):

Occupation - Farmer

Wedding Witnesses:

Joshua H. Roberts & Thomas Loftus

Signatures:

- John Loftus – b. 31 Mar 1870, bapt. 12 Jun 1870 (Baptism, **Aghold Parish**)

- Rachel Jane Loftus – b. 15 Apr 1873, bapt. 8 Jun 1873 (Baptism, **Aghold Parish**)

- Thomas Henry Loftus – b. 5 Apr 1877, bapt. 8 Jul 1877 (Baptism, **Aghold Parish**)

Richard Loftus (son):

Residence - Nickeen, Aghold Parish - December 1, 1859

November 11, 1860

Hurst

December 14, 1862

March 9, 1865

Rath - June 12, 1870

June 8, 1873

July 8, 1877

Occupation - Farmer - December 1, 1859

November 11, 1860

December 14, 1862

March 9, 1865

June 12, 1870

June 8, 1873

July 8, 1877

Mary Anne Codd, daughter of John Codd (daughter-in-law):

Residence - Munny, Aghold Parish - December 1, 1859

John Codd (father):

Occupation - Farmer

Richard Loftus (father):

Occupation - Farmer

Loftus Surname Ireland: 1600s to 1900s

Wedding Witnesses:

Edward Codd & John Codd

Signatures:

- o   Anne Loftus – b. 20 Jun 1841, bapt. 11 Jul 1841 (Baptism, **Aghold Parish**)

- o   Mary Loftus – b. 1 Aug 1843, bapt. 13 Aug 1843 (Baptism, **Aghold Parish**)

- o   Thomas Loftus – b. 25 Nov 1845, bapt. 14 Dec 1845 (Baptism, **Aghold Parish**)

Richard Loftus (father):

Residence - Rath or Knockeen - April 9, 1837

Knockeen - July 11, 1841

August 13, 1843

December 14, 1845

Occupation - Small Farmer - April 9, 1837

Farmer - July 11, 1841

August 13, 1843

Hurst

December 14, 1845

- Richard Loftus & Unknown
  - Henry Loftus, d. Bef. 26 Apr 1869 & Mary Loftus – 14 Dec 1857 (Marriage, **St. Michan Parish**)

Signatures:

Henry Loftus (son):

Residence - 37 Beresford Street - December 14, 1857

Occupation - Painter - December 14, 1857

Mary Loftus, daughter of Thomas Loftus (daughter-in-law):

Residence - 11 Coleraine Street - December 14, 1857

Thomas Loftus (father):

Occupation - Messenger

Richard Loftus (father):

Occupation - Painter

Wedding Witnesses:

Henry Graham & Thomas Loftus

Signatures:

- Richard Loftus & Unknown

  o Catherine Loftus & Abraham Pryce – 23 Oct 1886 (Marriage, **St. Stephen Parish**)

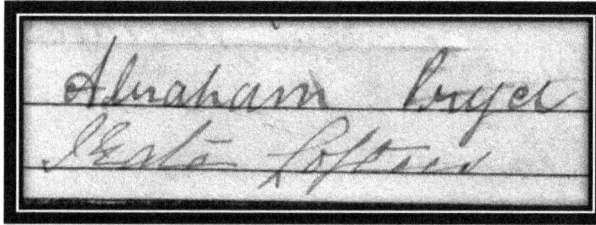

Signatures:

Catherine Loftus (daughter):

    Residence - 6 Merrion Place - October 23, 1886

Abraham Pryce, son of Samuel Pryce (son-in-law):

    Residence - Knocklow, Tullow Parish, Co. Carlow - October 23, 1886

    Occupation - Coachman - October 23, 1886

Samuel Pryce (father):

    Occupation - Farmer

Richard Loftus (father):

    Occupation - Farmer

Wedding Witnesses:

Margaret Mary Jewett & Elizabeth Howden

Signatures:

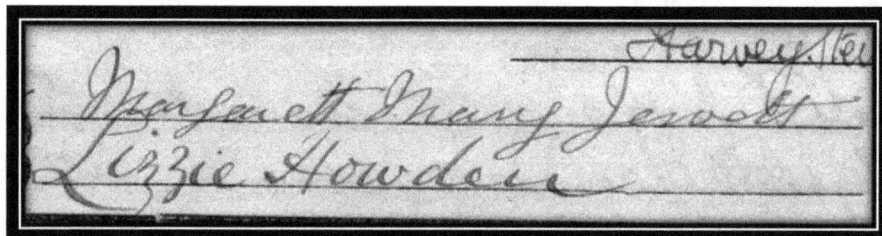

- Robert Loftus & Charlotte Kelly

  - Catherine Loftus – bapt. 18 Feb 1853 (Baptism, **St. Nicholas Parish (RC)**)

- Robert Loftus & Charlotte Quinn

  - Mary Loftus – b. 13 Mar 1857, bapt. 22 Mar 1857 (Baptism, **Rathmines Parish (RC)**)

  - Charlotte Loftus – b. 1 May 1859, bapt. 22 May 1859 (Baptism, **Rathmines Parish (RC)**)

  - Dennis Loftus – b. 25 Jun 1865, bapt. 10 Jul 1865 (Baptism, **St. Nicholas Parish (RC)**)

Robert Loftus (father):

Residence - Lock House, Charlemont Bridge - March 22, 1857

Charlemont Canal - May 22, 1859

43 Kevin Street - July 10, 1865

- Robert Loftus & Eleanor Goff

  - Mary Loftus – bapt. 8 Apr 1796 (Baptism, **St. Michan Parish (RC)**)

- Robert Loftus & Eleanor Keogh

  - Patrick Loftus – bapt. 9 Mar 1793 (Baptism, **St. Michan Parish (RC)**)

Loftus Surname Ireland: 1600s to 1900s

- Robert Loftus & Frances Unknown

  o Thomas Loftus – bapt. 17 Jan 1757 (Baptism, **St. Catherine Parish**)

- Robert Loftus & Rose Doherty

  o Mary Anne Loftus – bapt. 19 Sep 1851 (Baptism, **St. Catherine Parish** (RC))

- Samuel Loftus & Mary Loftus

  o Samuel Loftus – bapt. 19 Aug 1759 (Baptism, **St. Mary Parish**)

- Simon Loftus & Hannah Unknown

  o Arthur Loftus – bapt. Dec 1724 (Baptism, **St. John Parish**)

  o Dudley Loftus – bapt. 18 Oct 1730 (Baptism, **St. Mary Parish**)

Simon Loftus (father):

Occupation - Captain - October 18, 1739

- Simon Loftus & Mary Unknown

  o Mary Loftus – bapt. 16 Sep 1726 (Baptism, **St. Peter Parish**)

- Smyth Loftus & Sarah Loftus

  o Dudley Loftus – b. 22 May 1746, bapt. 1 Jun 1746 (Baptism, **St. Mary Parish**)

  o Alice Loftus – bapt. 3 Mar 1751 (Baptism, **St. Mary Parish**)

  o Thomas Loftus – bapt. 5 Aug 1752 (Baptism, **St. Mary Parish**)

Smyth Loftus (father):

Occupation - Reverend - March 3, 1751

August 5, 1752

Hurst

- Thomas Loftus & Alice Rochfort – 2 May 1734 (Marriage, **St. Mary Parish**)

Thomas Loftus (husband):

  Residence - Esquire - May 2, 1734

- Thomas Loftus & Amelia Underwood – 2 May 1831 (Marriage, **Tullow Parish**)

Signatures:

  ○ Mary Loftus (1st Marriage), b. 13 Jul 1832, bapt. 29 Jul 1832 (Baptism, **Tullow Parish**), b. 12 Jul 1832, bapt. 16 Apr 1878 (Baptism, **St. Mary. Pro Cathedral Parish (RC)**) & Henry Loftus, d. Bef. 26 Apr 1869 – 14 Dec 1857 (Marriage, **St. Michan Parish**)

Signatures:

Mary Loftus (daughter):

  Residence - 11 Coleraine Street - December 14, 1857

Henry Loftus, son of Richard Loftus (son-in-law):

  Residence - 37 Beresford Street - December 14, 1857

  Occupation - Painter - December 14, 1857

Loftus Surname Ireland: 1600s to 1900s

Richard Loftus (father):

   Occupation - Painter

Thomas Loftus (father):

   Occupation - Messenger

Wedding Witnesses:

Henry Graham & Thomas Loftus

Signatures:

- o Mary Loftus Loftus (2nd Marriage), b. 13 Jul 1832, bapt. 29 Jul 1832 (Baptism, **Tullow Parish**), b. 12 Jul 1832, bapt. 16 Apr 1878 (Baptism, **St. Mary. Pro Cathedral Parish (RC)**) & James Fay – 26 Apr 1869 (Marriage, **St. Thomas Parish**)

Signatures:

- ▪ Elizabeth Anne Fay – b. 6 Feb 1870, bapt. 14 Feb 1870 (Baptism, **St. Mary. Pro Cathedral Parish (RC)**)

Hurst

- Catherine Fay, b. 27 Jul 1872, bapt. 5 Aug 1872 (Baptism, **St. Mary. Pro Cathedral Parish (RC)**) & William Harris – 2 Jul 1892 (Marriage, **St. Mary. Pro Cathedral Parish (RC)**)

Catherine Fay (daughter):

Residence - 33 Upper Gloucester Place - July 2, 1892

William Harris, son of John Harris & Elizabeth Griffin (son-in-law):

Residence - 30 Mabbot Street - July 2, 1892

Wedding Witnesses:

James Cooke & Catherine Stephen

Mary Loftus Loftus (daughter):

Residence - 4 Gregg's Lane - April 26, 1869

Relationship Status at 2nd Marriage - widow

James Fay, son of Michael Fay (son-in-law):

Residence - 4 Gregg's Lane - April 26, 1869

August 5, 1872

Gregg's Lane - February 14, 1870

Occupation - Porter - April 26, 1869

Michael Fay (father):

Occupation - Coalman

Loftus Surname Ireland: 1600s to 1900s

Thomas Loftus (father):

Occupation - Messenger

Wedding Witnesses:

James Howard & Susan Quinn

Signatures:

- William Valentine Loftus – b. 17 Dec 1834, bapt. 25 Dec 1834 (Baptism, **Tullow Parish**)

- Thomas Loftus & Bridget Kearney (K e a r n e y) – 16 Mar 1868 (Marriage, **St. Mary Parish**)

Signature:

Signatures (Marriage):

Hurst

- Amelia Alice Loftus – b. 21 Aug 1864, bapt. 18 Sep 1867 (Baptism, **St. Mary Parish**)

- Emily Loftus – b. 21 Aug 1867, bapt. 7 Jun 1871 (Baptism, **St. Mary. Pro Cathedral Parish** (RC))

- John George Loftus – b. 5 May 1869, bapt. 18 Jun 1869 (Baptism, **St. Mary Parish**)

- Thomas Joseph Loftus – b. 16 Aug 1871, bapt. 21 Aug 1871 (Baptism, **St. Mary. Pro Cathedral Parish** (RC))

Thomas Loftus (son):

Residence - 12 Abbey Street - September 18, 1867

12 Middle Abbey Street - March 16, 1868

17 Upper Dorset Street - June 18, 1869

24 Gregg's Lane - June 7, 1871

25 Sackville Street - August 21, 1871

Occupation - Printer - September 18, 1867

March 16, 1868

Compositor - June 18, 1867

Bridget Kearney, daughter of Edward Kearney (daughter-in-law):

Residence - 12 Middle Abbey Street - March 16, 1868

Occupation - Brush Drawer - March 16, 1868

Edward Kearney (father):

Occupation - Butcher

Loftus Surname Ireland: 1600s to 1900s

Thomas Loftus (father):

    Occupation - Messenger

Wedding Witnesses:

James Hamard & Mary Loftus

Signatures:

Thomas Loftus (father):

    Residence - Tullow Parish - May 2, 1831

Amelia Underwood (mother):

    Residence - Tullow Parish - May 2, 1831

Wedding Witnesses:

James Byrne & Thomas Ralph

Signatures:

Hurst

- Thomas Loftus & Bridget Unknown

  o Anne Loftus – b. 27 Sep 1839, bapt. 29 Sep 1839 (Baptism, **St. Peter Parish**)

Thomas Loftus (father):

Residence - South King Street - September 29, 1839

- Thomas Loftus & Catherine Unknown

  o Timothy Loftus & Mary Goodby – 29 Sep 1873 (Marriage, **St. Nicholas Parish (RC)**)

    ▪ Mary Loftus – b. 12 Jan 1873, bapt. 20 Jan 1873 (Baptism, **St. Nicholas Parish (RC)**)

    ▪ Stephen Thomas Loftus – b. 24 Dec 1874, bapt. 28 Dec 1874 (Baptism, **St. Nicholas Parish (RC)**)

    ▪ Timothy Loftus – b. 20 Aug 1877, bapt. 30 Aug 1877 (Baptism, **St. Nicholas Parish (RC)**)

    ▪ Anne Loftus – b. 2 Jan 1881, bapt. 7 Jan 1881 (Baptism, **St. Nicholas Parish (RC)**)

Timothy Loftus (son):

Residence - 8 Draper's Court - January 20, 1873

12 Patrick Close - September 29, 1873

December 28, 1874

6 Francis Street - August 30, 1877

16 Bride's Alley - January 7, 1881

Mary Goodby, daughter of Samuel Goodby & Elizabeth Unknown (daughter-in-law):

Residence - 12 Patrick Close - September 29, 1873

Loftus Surname Ireland: 1600s to 1900s

Wedding Witnesses:

Thomas Loftus & Catherine Loftus

- Thomas Loftus & Emily Loftus

  o Frances Eleanor Loftus – b. 29 May 1840, bapt. 7 Jun 1840 (Baptism, **St. Werburgh Parish**)

- Thomas Loftus & Emily G. Allen

  o Emily Georgina Loftus – b. 17 May 1896, bapt. 29 May 1896 (Baptism, **St. Mary. Pro Cathedral Parish** (RC))

Thomas Loftus (father):

Residence - 27 Upper Gloucester Street - May 29, 1896

- Thomas Loftus & Jane Loftus

  o Anne Loftus – bapt. 9 Aug 1762 (Baptism, **St. Mary Parish**)

  o Mary Loftus – bapt. 18 Sep 1763 (Baptism, **St. Mary Parish**)

- Thomas Loftus & Mary Kavanagh

  o Bridget Loftus – bapt. 15 Sep 1848 (Baptism, **St. Catherine Parish** (RC))

- Thomas Loftus & Mary Kearney (K e a r n e y)

  o Timothy Loftus – bapt. 7 Dec 1849 (Baptism, **St. Catherine Parish** (RC))

- Thomas Loftus & Mary Loftus

  o Susanna Loftus – bapt. 17 Feb 1819 (Baptism, **Tullow Parish**)

- Thomas Loftus & Mary Underwood

  o Emily Loftus, bapt. 11 Jul 1896 (Baptism, **St. Mary. Pro Cathedral Parish** (RC)) & John Bryson – 11 Jul 1896 (Marriage, **St. Mary. Pro Cathedral Parish** (RC))

Hurst

Emily Loftus (daughter):

    Residence - 27 Upper Gloucester Street - July 11, 1896

    Age at Baptism - adult

John Bryson, son of Joseph Bryson & Julia Nolan (son-in-law):

    Residence - 27 Upper Gloucester Street - July 11, 1896

Wedding Witnesses:

William Harris & Catherine Harris

- Thomas Loftus & Mary Unknown
  - Anne Loftus & James Kelly – 6 May 1860 (Marriage, **St. Catherine Parish (RC)**)
    - Mary Kelly – b. 12 Feb 1861, bapt. 12 Feb 1861 (Baptism, **St. Catherine Parish (RC)**)
    - Catherine Kelly – b. 2 Oct 1863, bapt. 6 Oct 1863 (Baptism, **St. Catherine Parish (RC)**)
    - Teresa Kelly – b. 8 Mar 1868, bapt. 16 Mar 1868 (Baptism, **St. Nicholas Parish (RC)**)
    - Rosa Kelly – b. 27 Mar 1875, bapt. 7 Apr 1875 (Baptism, **St. Mary. Pro Cathedral Parish (RC)**)

Anne Loftus (daughter):

    Residence - 18 Cole Alley - May 6, 1860

James Kelly, son of John Kelly & Mary Unknown (son-in-law):

    Residence - 18 Cole Alley - May 6, 1860

        20 Pimlico - February 12, 1861

        9 Ormond Street - October 6, 1863

        16 Chancery Lane - March 16, 1868

Loftus Surname Ireland: 1600s to 1900s

47 Montgomery Street - April 7, 1875

Wedding Witnesses:

Thomas Hussey & Mary Brien

- Unknown Loftus & Elizabeth Loftus

    o Robert Loftus – b. 17 Feb 1887, bapt. 21 Feb 1887 (Baptism, **Aghold Parish**), bur. 18 Mar 1887 (Burial, **Aghold Parish**)

Robert Loftus (son):

Residence - Rath - before March 18, 1887

Age at Death - 1 month

Unknown Loftus (father):

Residence - Rath - February 21, 1887

Occupation - Farmer - February 21, 1887

- Unknown Loftus & Emily Loftus

    o Mary Jane Loftus – b. 7 Oct 1881, bapt. 24 Oct 1881 (Baptism, **St. Mary. Pro Cathedral Parish (RC)**)

Emily Loftus (mother):

Residence - 4 Gregg's Lane otherwise Finlater's Place - October 24, 1881

- Unknown Loftus & Jane Loftus

    o Stephen Loftus Giles Loftus – b. 31 Mar 1898, bapt. 3 Apr 1898 (Baptism, **Rotunda Chapel Parish**)

Hurst

Jane Loftus (mother):

Residence - 33 Lower Gardiner Street - April 3, 1898

- Unknown Loftus & Mary Loftus
  - Anne Loftus – bapt. 26 Feb 1801 (Baptism, **Cork - South Parish (RC)**)

Unknown Loftus (father):

Occupation - Captain, 16th Regiment - February 26, 1801

- Unknown Loftus & Unknown
  - Adam Robert Charles Loftus & Margaret Fannin – 11 Jun 1846 (Marriage, **St. Peter Parish**)

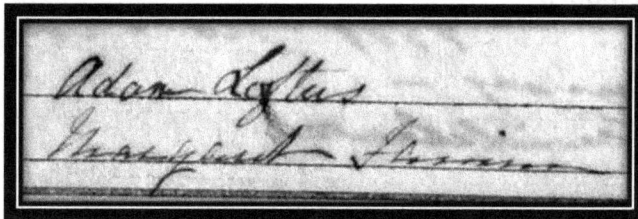

Signatures:

- Mary Anne Loftus – b. 6 Dec 1849, bapt. 31 Jan 1850 (Baptism, **St. Peter Parish**)

Adam Robert Charles Loftus (husband):

Residence - Ely Lodge, Ennisville - June 11, 1846

Ar Dass Glebe - January 31, 1850

Occupation - Clergyman - June 11, 1846

Clerk - January 31, 1850

Margaret Fannin, daughter of Robert Fannin (daughter-in-law):

Residence - Leeson Street - June 11, 1846

Robert Fannin (father):

    Occupation - Esquire

Unknown Loftus (father):

    Title - Marquis of Ely

Wedding Witnesses:

Anne Loftus, Catherine Loftus, Charlotte Knox, & Henry Loftus

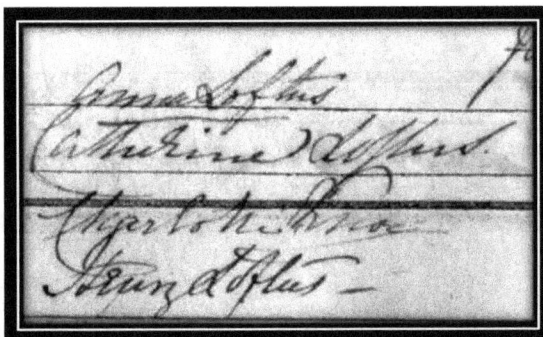

Signatures:

- Unknown Loftus & Unknown

  - Anne Loftus

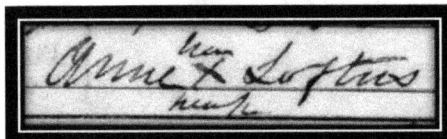

Signature:

- Unknown Loftus & Unknown

  o Anne Loftus

Signature:

- Unknown Loftus & Unknown

  o Catherine Loftus

Signature:

- Unknown Loftus & Unknown

  o Elizabeth Loftus

Signature:

- Unknown Loftus & Unknown

  o James Loftus

Signatures:

- Unknown Loftus & Unknown

  o John Loftus

Signature:

- Unknown Loftus & Unknown

  o John Loftus

Signature:

Hurst

- Unknown Loftus & Unknown

  o Thomas Loftus

Signature:

- Unknown Loftus & Unknown

  o Thomas Loftus

Signature:

- Valentine Loftus & Alice Loftus

  o Valentine Loftus – bapt. 26 Apr 1807 (Baptism, **Tullow Parish**)

- Valentine Loftus & Catherine Loftus

  o Valentine Loftus – bapt. 23 Nov 1840 (Baptism, **St. Michan Parish** (RC))

  o Valentine Loftus – bapt. 23 Nov 1841 (Baptism, **St. Michan Parish** (RC))

- Valentine Loftus & Eleanor Loftus

  o Ellen Loftus – b. 2 Aug 1827, bapt. 12 Aug 1827 (Baptism, **Tullow Parish**)

- Valentine Loftus & Elizabeth Loftus

  o Richard Loftus, bapt. 17 May 1818 (Baptism, **Tullow Parish**), bur. 14 Oct 1893 (Burial,

  Urglin Parish) & Elizabeth Coleman, b. 1828, bur. 21 Feb 1911 (Burial, **Urglin Parish**) –

  27 Feb 1854 (Marriage, **Urglin Parish**)

Loftus Surname Ireland: 1600s to 1900s

Signatures:

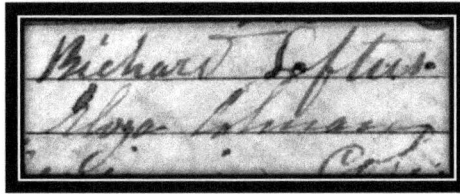

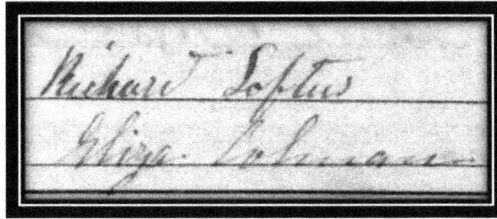

- Richard Benjamin Loftus – b. 25 Nov 1854, bapt. 21 Feb 1855 (Baptism, **Urglin Parish**)

- William Loftus – bapt. 4 May 1856 (Baptism, **Urglin Parish**), bur. 10 Oct 1858 (Burial, **Urglin Parish**)

William Loftus (son):

Residence - Palatine - before October 10, 1858

Age at Death - 2 ½ years

- Samuel Loftus – bapt. 7 Jun 1857 (Baptism, **Urglin Parish**)

- James Loftus – bapt. 25 Jul 1858 (Baptism, **Urglin Parish**)

- Elizabeth Loftus – bapt. 12 Feb 1860 (Baptism, **Urglin Parish**)

- Anne Loftus – bapt. 17 May 1862 (Baptism, **Urglin Parish**)

- William Loftus – bapt. 24 Aug 1865 (Baptism, **Urglin Parish**), bur. 10 Mar 1884 (Burial, **Urglin Parish**)

Hurst

William Loftus (son):

Residence - Palatine - before March 10, 1884

Age at Death - 19 years

- ▪ John Loftus, b. 8 Jun 1869, bapt. 12 Sep 1869 (Baptism, **Urglin Parish**) & Florence Goldie

  Ashmore – 28 Nov 1892 (Marriage, **Urglin Parish**)

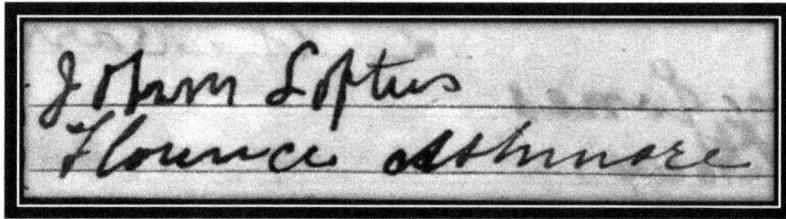

Signatures:

- Anne Loftus – b. 27 Sep 1893, bapt. 5 Nov 1893 (Baptism, **Urglin Parish**)

- John Benjamin Loftus – b. 29 Sep 1895, bapt. 1 Dec 1895 (Baptism, **Urglin Parish**)

- Harriet Augusta Loftus – b. 25 Mar 1897, bapt. 20 Jun 1897 (Baptism, **Urglin Parish**)

- Samuel Loftus – b. 7 May 1898, bapt. 7 Aug 1898 (Baptism, **Urglin Parish**)

- Florence Susan Loftus – b. 1901, bur. 25 Mar 1915 (Burial, **Urglin Parish**)

Florence Susan Loftus (daughter):

Residence - Knockdane 60 Kildan - before March 25, 1915

Age at Death - 14 years

- Elizabeth Loftus – bur. 22 Oct 1919 (Burial, **Urglin Parish**)

Elizabeth Loftus (daughter):

Residence - Knockbawn Palatine - before October 22, 1919

Loftus Surname Ireland: 1600s to 1900s

John Loftus (son):

Residence - Palatine - November 28, 1892

Knockbawn Ballyhade - November 5, 1893

Knockvann - December 1, 1895

June 20, 1897

August 7, 1898

Occupation - Farmer - November 28, 1892

November 5, 1893

December 1, 1895

June 20, 1897

August 7, 1898

Florence Goldie Ashmore, daughter of John Goldie (daughter-in-law):

Residence - Knockbane - November 28, 1892

Occupation - Farmer - November 28, 1892

Relationship Status at Marriage - widow

John Goldie (father):

Occupation - Farmer

Richard Loftus (father):

Occupation - Shopkeeper

Hurst

Wedding Witnesses:

Samuel Watchorn & Anne Meara

Signatures:

Richard Loftus (son):

    Residence - Palatine, Urglin Parish - February 27, 1854

                February 21, 1855

                May 4, 1856

                June 7, 1857

                July 25, 1858

                February 12, 1860

                May 17, 1862

                August 24, 1865

                September 12, 1869

                before October 14, 1893

    Occupation - Shopkeeper - February 27, 1854

                February 21, 1855

                May 4, 1856

Loftus Surname Ireland: 1600s to 1900s

June 7, 1857

July 25, 1858

February 12, 1860

May 17, 1862

August 24, 1865

Farmer - September 12, 1869

Age at Death - 76 years

Elizabeth Coleman, daughter of Benjamin Coleman (daughter-in-law):

Residence - Killeshane, Urglin Parish - February 27, 1854

Palatine - before February 21, 1911

Age at Death - 83 years

Benjamin Coleman (father):

Occupation - Farmer

Valentine Loftus (father):

Occupation - Farmer

Wedding Witnesses:

Benjamin Coleman & John Murphy

Signatures:

- o   James Loftus – bapt. 24 Jun 1821 (Baptism, **Tullow Parish**)

- o   Margaret E. Loftus, bapt. 15 Feb 1824 (Baptism, **Tullow Parish**) & Francis Philips – 28 Apr

    1846 (Marriage, **Aghold Parish**)

Signatures:

Margaret E. Loftus (daughter):

   Residence - Knocklow, Aghold Parish - April 28, 1846

Loftus Surname Ireland: 1600s to 1900s

Francis Philips, son of Francis Philips (son-in-law):

Residence - Coppenagh, Tullow Parish - April 28, 1846

Occupation - Farmer - April 28, 1846

Francis Philips (father):

Occupation - Farmer

Valentine Loftus (father):

Occupation - Farmer

Wedding Witnesses:

James Loftus & Richard Loftus

Signatures:

- o   Mary Anne Loftus – b. 10 Jan 1832, bapt. 22 Jan 1832 (Baptism, **Tullow Parish**)

- o   Valentine Loftus – b. 5 Nov 1834, bapt. 16 Nov 1834 (Baptism, **Aghold Parish**)

Hurst

- Valentine Loftus & Mary D'Arcy

  - Thomas Loftus, b. 1851, bapt. 4 Jun 1885 (Baptism, **St. Mary, Haddington Road Parish (RC)**) & Margaret Molloy – 8 Jun 1885 (Marriage, **St. Mary. Pro Cathedral Parish (RC)**)

    - Patrick Loftus – b. 1886, bapt. 1886 (Baptism, **St. Andrew Parish (RC)**)

    - Mary Jane Loftus – b. 1888, bapt. 1888 (Baptism, **St. Andrew Parish (RC)**)

Thomas Loftus (son):

Residence - Church Town, Co. Dublin - June 4, 1885

9 Green Street - June 8, 1885

14 Nassau Place - 1886

4 Mark's Street - 1888

Age at Baptism - adult

Margaret Molloy, daughter of Patrick Molloy & Margaret Gallegan

(daughter-in-law):

Residence - 9 Green Street - June 8, 1885

Wedding Witnesses:

John Breen & Bridget Breen

- Valentine Loftus & Mary Murphy

  - Susan Loftus – bapt. 1896 (Baptism, **St. Andrew Parish (RC)**)

Loftus Surname Ireland: 1600s to 1900s

Valentine Loftus (father):

Residence - Ring's End - 1896

- William Loftus & Anne Loftus
    - John Loftus – bapt. 6 Feb 1825 (Baptism, **Tullow Parish**)
    - Ellen Loftus – b. 3 Apr 1828, bapt. 11 Apr 1828 (Baptism, **Tullow Parish**)
- William Loftus & Catherine Field
    - John Loftus – bapt. 5 Feb 1769 (Baptism, **St. Catherine Parish (RC)**)
- William Loftus & Elizabeth Loftus
    - William Loftus – bapt. 26 Aug 1821 (Baptism, **Tullow Parish**)
- William Loftus & Frances Loftus
    - William Loftus – bapt. 14 Dec 1845 (Baptism, **Aghold Parish**)
    - John Loftus – b. 24 Aug 1847, bapt. 21 Sep 1847 (Baptism, **Carlow Parish**)
    - Anne Loftus – b. 8 Jun 1850, bapt. 3 Jul 1850 (Baptism, **Carlow Parish**)

William Loftus (father):

Residence - Knockeen - December 14, 1845

Carlow - September 21, 1847

July 3, 1850

Occupation - Servant & Laborer - December 14, 1845

Labourer - September 21, 1847

July 3, 1850

Hurst

- William Loftus & Mary King – 19 Feb 1778 (Marriage, **St. Mary Parish**)

William Loftus (father):

Occupation - Lieutenant, 3ʳᵈ Regiment of Guards - February 19, 1778

Individual Baptisms/Births

- Anne Loftus – b. 30 May 1760, bapt. Unclear (Baptism, **St. Paul Parish**)

- John Loftus – bapt. 28 May 1822 (Baptism, **St. Mary. Pro Cathedral Parish (RC)**)

John Loftus (child):

Remarks about Birth - foundling

- Mary Loftus – bapt. 7 Apr 1823 (Baptism, **St. Mary. Pro Cathedral Parish (RC)**)

Mary Loftus (child):

Residence - Loftus Lane - April 7, 1823

Remarks about Birth - foundling

- Mary Loftus – b. 19 Jun 1877, bapt. 24 Jun 1877 (Baptism, **Killarney Parish (RC)**)

Individual Burials

- Adam Loftus – b. 1854, d. 20 Jan 1866, bur. Unclear (Burial, **St. James Parish**)

Adam Loftus (deceased):

    Residence - No. 3 Marine Terrace - January 20, 1866

    Age at Death - 12 years

- Anne Loftus – b. 1755, bur. 6 Jan 1825 (Burial, **St. Mary Parish**)

Anne Loftus (deceased):

    Residence - Leeson Street - before January 6, 1825

    Age at Death - 70 years

    Relationship Status at Death - Mrs.

- Anne Loftus – b. 1835, bur. 13 Aug 1840 (Burial, **Aghold Parish**)

Anne Loftus (deceased):

    Residence - Knocklow or Knockeen - before August 13, 1840

    Age at Death - 5 years

- Anne Loftus – b. 1796, bur. 6 Jan 1853 (Burial, **Aghold Parish**)

Anne Loftus (deceased):

    Residence - Knocklow - before January 6, 1853

Loftus Surname Ireland: 1600s to 1900s

Age At Death - 57 years

- Arthur Loftus – d. 14 Sep 1659, bur. 16 Sep 1659 (Burial, **St. Patrick Parish**)

Arthur Loftus (deceased):

Social Status - Sir

Place of Burial - Loftus Vault - September 16, 1659

- Buckley Loftus – bur. 12 Mar 1786 (Burial, **St. Peter Parish**)

Buckley Loftus (deceased):

Residence - Montgomery - before March 12, 1786

- Dudley Loftus – bur. 9 Aug 1805 (Burial, **St. Mary Parish**)

Dudley Loftus (deceased):

Residence - Henry Street - before August 9, 1805

- Edward Loftus – bur. 1 Jun 1784 (Burial, **St. Paul Parish**)

- Elizabeth Loftus – bur. 14 Jul 1788 (Burial, **St. Paul Parish**)

- Elizabeth Loftus – bur. 30 Sep 1788 (Burial, **St. Paul Parish**)

- Elizabeth Loftus – b. 1814, bur. 25 Mar 1847 (Burial, **Aghold Parish**)

Elizabeth Loftus (deceased):

Residence - Knockeen - before March 25, 1847

Age at Death - 33 years

Hurst

- James Loftus – b. Jan 1828, bur. 24 Sep 1828 (Burial, **St. Mark Parish**)

James Loftus (deceased):

Residence - Townsend Street - before September 24, 1828

Age at Death - 8 months

- John Loftus – b. 1797, bur. 26 Apr 1847 (Burial, **St. Luke Parish**)

John Loftus (deceased):

Residence - Cork Street Hospital - before April 26, 1847

Age at Death - 50 years

- John Loftus – b. 1824, bur. 20 Apr 1873 (Burial, **Aghold Parish**)

John Loftus (father):

Residence - Rath - before April 20, 1873

Age at Death - 49 years

- Margaret Loftus – bur. 27 Mar 1723 (Burial, **St. Nicholas Without Parish**)

Margaret Loftus (deceased):

Residence - The Poddle - before March 27, 1723

- Margaret Loftus – b. 1832, bur. 28 Sep 1835 (Burial, **St. Peter Parish**)

Margaret Loftus (deceased):

Residence - Fearon Court - before September 28, 1835

Age at Death - 3 years

Loftus Surname Ireland: 1600s to 1900s

Place of Burial - St. Kevin's Cemetery

- Margaret Loftus – b. 1816, bur. 17 Oct 1859 (Burial, **Aghold Parish**)

Margaret Loftus (deceased):

Residence - Knockeen - before October 17, 1859

Age at Death - 43 years

- Mary Loftus – bur. 4 Oct 1721 (Burial, **St. Nicholas Without Parish**)

Mary Loftus (deceased):

Residence - Garden Lane - before October 4, 1721

- Mary Loftus – bur. 27 Oct 1726 (Burial, **St. Peter Parish**)

- Mary Loftus – bur. 18 May 1739 (Burial, **St. Catherine Parish**)

- Mary Loftus – b. 1762, bur. 10 Sep 1829 (Burial, **Glasnevin Parish**)

Mary Loftus (deceased):

Residence - Circular Road - before September 10, 1829

Age at Death - 67 years

- Mary Loftus – b. 1783, bur. 23 Jun 1865 (Burial, **Aghold Parish**)

Mary Loftus (deceased):

Residence - Castlemacadam Parish - before June 23, 1865

Age at Death - 82 years

Hurst

- Mary Loftus – b. 1808, bur. 26 Aug 1878 (Burial, **Taney Parish**)

Mary Loftus (deceased):

    Residence - Ballinteer - before August 26, 1878

    Age at Death - 70 years

- Mary Loftus – b. 1801, bur. 13 Feb 1885 (Burial, **Aghold Parish**)

Mary Loftus (deceased):

    Residence - Rath - before February 13, 1885

    Age at Death - 84 years

- Mary Matilda Loftus – b. 1759, bur. 22 Apr 1852 (Burial, **St. Peter Parish**)

Mary Matilda Loftus (deceased):

    Residence - Northumberland Road - before April 22, 1852

    Age at Death - 93 years

- Nicholas Loftus – bur. 7 Apr 1708 (Burial, **St. Patrick Parish**)

Nicholas Loftus (deceased):

    Occupation - Esquire - before April 7, 1708

- Patrick Loftus – b. 1840, bur. 4 May 1847 (Burial, **St. Luke Parish**)

Patrick Loftus (deceased):

    Residence - Cork Street Hospital - before May 4, 1847

    Age at Death - 7 years

Loftus Surname Ireland: 1600s to 1900s

- Richard Loftus – bur. 15 Feb 1768 (Burial, **St. Mark Parish**)

Richard Loftus (deceased):

> **Residence - Fleet Street - before February 15, 1768**

- Richard Loftus – b. 1795, bur. 20 Dec 1847 (Burial, **Aghold Parish**)

Richard Loftus (deceased):

> **Residence - Knockeen - before December 20, 1847**

> **Age At Death - 52 years**

- Richard Loftus – b. 1819, bur. 17 Mar 1854 (Burial, **Dunleckney Parish**)

Richard Loftus (deceased):

> **Residence - Royal Oak - before March 17, 1854**

> **Age at Death - 35 years**

- Richard Loftus – b. 1801, bur. 7 Aug 1858 (Burial, **Aghold Parish**)

Richard Loftus (deceased):

> **Residence - Knockeen - before August 7, 1858**

> **Age At Death - 57 years**

- Robert Loftus – bur. 30 Nov 1799 (Burial, **Glasnevin Parish**)

Robert Loftus (deceased):

> **Residence - Road - before November 30, 1799**

> **Remarks About Death - probably died while travelling on a road.**

Hurst

- Robert Loftus – b. 1758, bur. 25 May 1831 (Burial, **Glasnevin Parish**)

Robert Loftus (deceased):

    Residence - Phipsborough - before May 25, 1831

    Age at Death - 73 years

- Samuel Loftus – bur. 24 Oct 1709 (Baptism, **St. Catherine Parish**)

- Thomas Loftus – bur. 8 Sep 1794 (Burial, **St. Paul Parish**)

- Thomas Loftus – b. 1815, bur. 17 May 1840 (Burial, **Aghold Parish**)

Thomas Loftus (deceased):

    Residence - Celbridge - before May 17, 1840

    Age at Death - 25 years

- Thomas Loftus – b. 1784, bur. 1 Nov 1850 (Burial, **Aghold Parish**)

Thomas Loftus (deceased):

    Residence - Ballinabarney - before November 1, 1850

    Age at Death - 66 years

- Thomas Loftus – b. 1836, d. 3 Aug 1855, bur. 4 Aug 1855 (Burial, **Arbour Hill Barracks Parish**)

Thomas Loftus (deceased):

    Occupation - Drummer, 56th Regiment - August 3, 1855

    Age at Death - 19 years

    Cause of Death - phshisis pulmanalis

Loftus Surname Ireland: 1600s to 1900s

- Unknown Loftus – bur. 13 Sep 1738 (Burial, **St. Nicholas Without Parish**)

Unknown Loftus (deceased):

Residence - St. Bridget Parish - before September 13, 1738

- Unknown Loftus – bur. 29 Oct 1709 (Burial, **St. Patrick Parish**)

Unknown Loftus (deceased):

Social Status - Lady

Place of Burial - "in the Choir" - October 29, 1709

- Unknown Loftus (Mr.) – bur. 6 Aug 1761 (Burial, **St. Mary Parish**)

Unknown Loftus (Mr.) (deceased):

Residence - Henry Street - before August 6, 1761

- Unknown Loftus (Mr.) – 3 Jan 1764 (Burial, **St. Mary Parish**)

Unknown Loftus (Mr.) (deceased):

Remarks About Death - the church register entry refers to this man

as the "Right Honorable Lord Loftus".

- Unknown Loftus (Mrs.) – 21 Feb 1765 (Burial, **St. Mary Parish**)
- Valentine Loftus – b. 1835, bur. 4 Oct 1842 (Burial, **Aghold Parish**)

Valentine Loftus (deceased):

Residence - Knocklow - before October 4, 1842

Age at Death - 7 years

Individual Marriages

- Alice Loftus & Martin Mallen

  o Patrick Mallen & Catherine Newman – 1 Feb 1891 (Marriage, **St. Mary. Pro Cathedral Parish (RC)**)

Patrick Mallen (son):

Residence - 43 Middle Abbey Street - February 1, 1891

Catherine Newman, daughter of Joseph Newman & Catherine Cambe

(daughter-in-law):

Residence - 113 Middle Abbey Street - February 1, 1891

Wedding Witnesses:

Patrick Killeen & Jane Mowls

- Alice Loftus & Patrick Roberts

  o Catherine Roberts – b. 1 Jul 1875, bapt. 19 Jul 1875 (Baptism, **St. Michan Parish (RC)**)

Patrick Roberts (father):

Residence - 4 North Anne Street - July 19, 1875

- Anne Loftus & Francis Browne

  o Anne Jane Browne – b. 15 Sep 1875, bapt. 17 Sep 1875 (Baptism, **St. Michan Parish (RC)**)

Loftus Surname Ireland: 1600s to 1900s

Francis Browne (father):

Residence - 29 Eccles Lane - September 17, 1875

- Anne Loftus & Loftus Hayden
  - Patrick Hayden – b. 23 Jul 1898, bapt. 25 Jul 1898 (Baptism, **St. Mary. Pro Cathedral Parish (RC)**)

Loftus Hayden (father):

Residence - 13 Upper Tyrone Street - July 25, 1898

- Bridget Loftus & Charles Beake
  - George Beake – b. 25 Mar 1864, bapt. 1 Apr 1864 (Baptism, **St. Audoen Parish (RC)**)

Charles Beake (father):

Residence - Ship Street Barrack - April 1, 1864

- Bridget Loftus & James Rigney
  - Bridget Rigney – bapt. 21 Jan 1851 (Baptism, **St. Catherine Parish (RC)**)
  - John Rigney – b. 28 Oct 1859, bapt. 4 Nov 1859 (Baptism, **St. Nicholas Parish (RC)**)

James Rigney (father):

Residence - 7 Patrick Street - November 4, 1859

- Bridget Loftus & Michael Brennan
  - Hugh Brennan – bapt. 13 Dec 1825 (Baptism, **St. Michan Parish (RC)**)
- Bridget Loftus & Patrick Burke
  - John Burke & Margaret Smith – 10 Oct 1858 (Marriage, **St. Catherine Parish (RC)**)

Hurst

John Burke (son):

    Residence - **27 White's Lane - October 10, 1858**

Margaret Smith, daughter of James Smith & Bridget English (son-in-law):

    Residence - **5 Gibraltar - October 10, 1858**

Wedding Witnesses:

Richard Cunningham & Anne Scott

- Bridget Loftus & Patrick Kelly

  - Eleanor Kelly – b. 31 Oct 1823, bapt. 14 Nov 1823 (Baptism, **St. Catherine Parish (RC)**)

- Catherine Loftus & Dennis O'Neil

  - Charles O'Neil – bapt. 3 Nov 1800 (Baptism, **St. Catherine Parish (RC)**)

- Catherine Loftus & George Rich

  - Cecilia Rich – bapt. 9 Oct 1862 (Baptism, **St. Mary. Pro Cathedral Parish (RC)**)

George Rich (father):

    Residence - **8 Cavendish Row - October 9, 1862**

- Christine Loftus & Gregory Doyle

  - Gregory Doyle & Anne Lowry – 7 May 1863 (Marriage, **St. Andrew Parish (RC)**)

Gregory Doyle (son):

    Residence - **Bray - May 7, 1863**

Anne Lowry, daughter of Peter Lowry & Mary Handler (daughter-in-law):

    Residence - **Fitzwilliam Square - May 7, 1863**

Loftus Surname Ireland: 1600s to 1900s

Wedding Witnesses:

Thomas Kirkley & Elizabeth Kenny

- Eleanor Loftus & Michael Dungan

    o Catherine Dungan – bapt. 6 Nov 1833 (Baptism, **St. Nicholas Parish (RC)**)

    o Bridget Dungan – bapt. 22 Jan 1839 (Baptism, **St. Nicholas Parish (RC)**)

    o Patrick Dungan – bapt. 26 Feb 1841 (Baptism, **St. Nicholas Parish (RC)**)

    o Mary Dungan – bapt. 16 Apr 1843 (Baptism, **St. Nicholas Parish (RC)**)

    o Ellen Dungan – bapt. 12 Nov 1847 (Baptism, **St. Nicholas Parish (RC)**)

- Elizabeth Loftus & John Dunne – 29 Jul 1850 (Marriage, **St. Mary Parish (RC)**)

Wedding Witnesses:

William Sullivan & Elizabeth Murphy

- Elizabeth Loftus & John Healy

    o Edward Patrick Healy – b. 28 Feb 1874, bapt. 2 Mar 1874 (Baptism, **SS. Michael & John Parish (RC)**)

John Healy (father):

Residence - 9 Wine Tavern Street - March 2, 1874

- Elizabeth Loftus & Joseph Ellis – 14 Dec 1733 (Marriage, **St. Nicholas Without Parish**)
- Elizabeth Loftus & Thomas Hassett

    o Elizabeth Hassett – b. 4 May 1827, bapt. 4 May 1827 (Baptism, **Killarney Parish (RC)**)

Thomas Hassett (father):

Residence - Killarney - May 4, 1827

Hurst

- Ellen Loftus & Dennis Buckley

  o Dennis Buckley – b. 27 Sep 1867, bapt. 30 Sep 1867 (Baptism, **St. Michan Parish** (RC))

  o Jane Buckley – b. 17 May 1871, bapt. 19 May 1871 (Baptism, **St. Michan Parish** (RC))

  o Joseph Buckley – b. 20 Sep 1873, bapt. 24 Sep 1873 (Baptism, **St. Michan Parish** (RC))

Dennis Buckley (father):

Residence - 7 Bull Lane - September 30, 1867

61 Mary's Lane - May 19, 1871

17 Fisher Lane - September 24, 1873

- Ellen Loftus & Michael Hogan

  o Dennis Hogan – b. 22 Oct 1813, bapt. 22 Oct 1813 (Baptism, **Killarney Parish** (RC))

Michael Hogan (father):

Residence - Bunraur - October 22, 1813

- Emily Loftus & John Clarke

  o John Henry Clarke – b. 30 Jan 1880, bapt. 9 Feb 1880 (Baptism, **St. Mary. Pro Cathedral Parish** (RC))

John Clarke (father):

Residence - 4 Gregg's Lane - February 9, 1880

- Hannah Loftus & Henry Codd – 29 May 1835 (Marriage, **Aghold Parish**)

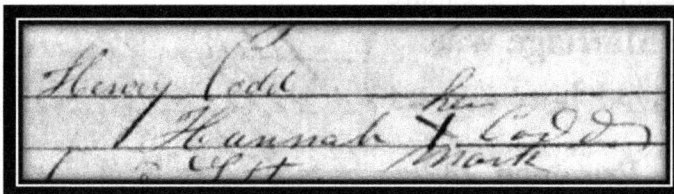

Signatures:

Hannah Loftus (wife):

  Residence - Liscolman Parish - May 29, 1835

Henry Codd (husband):

  Residence - Liscolman Parish - May 29, 1835

Wedding Witnesses:

Richard Loftus & James Beckett

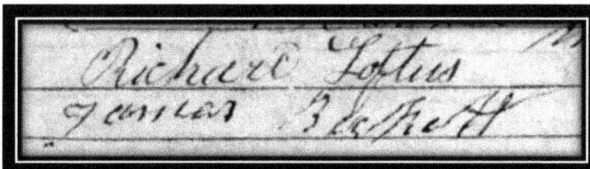

Signatures:

- Jane Loftus & Edward Brown – 26 Dec 1746 (Marriage, **St. Catherine Parish (RC)**)

Wedding Witnesses:

Catherine Brown & Mary Sullivan

- Jane Loftus & John Rose

  o Joshua Rose – b. 8 Feb 1900, bapt. 23 Feb 1900 (Baptism, **Kiltennel Parish**)

Hurst

Joshua Rose (son):

    Remarks about Birth - illegitimate

John Rose (father):

    Residence - Coonogue - February 23, 1900

    Occupation - Farmer - February 23, 1900

- Jane Loftus & Thomas Hughes – Sep 1818 (Marriage, **St. Michan Parish** (RC))

    o Mary Hughes – bapt. May 1819 (Baptism, **St. Michan Parish** (RC))

    o Eleanor Hughes – bapt. 14 May 1821 (Baptism, **St. Michan Parish** (RC))

Wedding Witnesses:

Jane Doyle & Mary Murphy

- Margaret Loftus & Edward Murphy – 2 May 1744 (Marriage, **St. Andrew Parish** (RC))

Wedding Witnesses:

James Dorney & Bridget Dorney

- Margaret Loftus & Timothy Riordan

    o Michael Riordan – b. 23 Mar 1858, bapt. 23 Mar 1858 (Baptism, **Dromod Parish** (RC))

    o John Loftus Riordan – b. 24 Jun 1859, bapt. 24 Jun 1859 (Baptism, **Dromod Parish** (RC))

    o Margaret Riordan – b. 6 Apr 1861, bapt. 6 Apr 1861 (Baptism, **Dromod Parish** (RC))

    o Bridget Riordan – b. 10 Dec 1863, bapt. 10 Dec 1863 (Baptism, **Dromod Parish** (RC))

    o Timothy Michael Riordan – b. 31 Dec 1866, bapt. 31 Dec 1866 (Baptism, **Dromod Parish** (RC))

Loftus Surname Ireland: 1600s to 1900s

Timothy Loftus (father):

Residence - Waterville - March 23, 1858

June 24, 1859

April 6, 1861

December 10, 1863

December 31, 1866

- Mary Loftus & Cornelius (C o r n e l i u s) Cotter – 13 Apr 1839 (Marriage, **Cork - SS. Peter & Paul Parish** (RC))

Wedding Witnesses:

Daniel Ford & Anne Cotter

- Mary Loftus & Darby Murphy
  - Judith Murphy – bapt. 30 Apr 1780 (Baptism, **St. Catherine Parish** (RC))
  - Michael Murphy – bapt. 31 Aug 1787 (Baptism, **St. Catherine Parish** (RC))
- Mary Loftus & Eugene Riordan – 17 Nov 1811 (Marriage, **Killarney Parish** (RC))
  - Dennis Riordan – b. 24 Jan 1813, bapt. 24 Jan 1813 (Baptism, **Killarney Parish** (RC))
  - Joan Riordan – b. 10 Jun 1814, bapt. 10 Jun 1814 (Baptism, **Killarney Parish** (RC))
  - Mary Riordan – b. 8 Dec 1816, bapt. 8 Dec 1816 (Baptism, **Killarney Parish** (RC))
  - Honor Riordan – b. 12 Sep 1819, bapt. 12 Sep 1819 (Baptism, **Killarney Parish** (RC))
  - Elizabeth Riordan – b. 22 Sep 1822, bapt. 22 Sep 1822 (Baptism, **Killarney Parish** (RC))

Mary Loftus (mother):

Residence - Killarney - November 17, 1811

Hurst

December 8, 1816

September 12, 1819

September 22, 1822

Eugene Riordan (father):

Residence - Killarney - November 17, 1811

January 23, 1813

Wedding Witnesses:

Jeremiah Sullivan & Patrick Sullivan

- Mary Loftus & Henry Allen
  - Henry Allen, b. 21 May 1861, bapt. 11 May 1885 (Baptism, St. Mary. Pro Cathedral Parish (RC)) & Martha Caffrey – 21 Jan 1884 (Marriage, St. Mary. Pro Cathedral Parish (RC))

Henry Allen (son):

Residence - 143 Great Britain Street - January 21, 1884

7 Gardiner's Lane - May 11, 1885

Age at Baptism - adult

Remarks about Baptism - private baptism, an adult convert

Martha Caffrey, daughter of Thomas Caffrey & Mary Keane (daughter-in-law):

Residence - 1 Moore Place - January 21, 1884

Loftus Surname Ireland: 1600s to 1900s

Wedding Witnesses:

John Cafferty & Mary White

- Mary Loftus & James McNamara

    - Martin McNamara – bapt. 30 May 1830 (Baptism, **St. Catherine Parish (RC)**)

    - James McNamara – bapt. 11 Dec 1831 (Baptism, **St. Catherine Parish (RC)**)

- Mary Loftus & John Arington – 7 Jul 1761 (Marriage, **St. Werburgh Parish**)

- Mary Loftus & Patrick Kennedy – 11 Oct 1849 (Marriage, **St. Catherine Parish (RC)**)

Wedding Witnesses:

Patrick Jordan & Mary Loftus

- Mary Loftus & Richard Butler – 16 Sep 1703 (Marriage, **St. Michan Parish**)

Richard Butler (husband):

Occupation - Butcher - September 16, 1703

- Mary Loftus & Richard Molloy

    - Anne Molloy & Francis Broe – 10 Feb 1873 (Marriage, **St. Andrew Parish (RC)**)

        - John Joseph Broe – b. 1873, bapt. 1873 (Baptism, **St. Andrew Parish (RC)**)

        - Margaret Mary Broe – b. 1878, bapt. 1878 (Baptism, **St. Andrew Parish (RC)**)

        - Francis Broe – b. 1880, bapt. 1880 (Baptism, **St. Andrew Parish (RC)**)

        - Ellen Broe – b. 1882, bapt. 1882 (Baptism, **St. Andrew Parish (RC)**)

Anne Molloy (daughter):

Residence - 9 Egan Court - February 10, 1873

Hurst

Francis Broe, son of John Broe & Ellen Unknown (son-in-law):

Residence - 3 Merrion Place - February 10, 1873

1873

11 Mackey's Terrace - 1878

48 Power's Court - 1880

1 Mackey's Terrace, Quinn's Lane - 1882

Wedding Witnesses:

George Pritchard & Jane Flood

- Mary Loftus & Russell Doran
  - o Francis Russell Doran – bapt. 9 Apr 1849 (Baptism, St. James Parish (RC))
- Mary Loftus & Thomas Boyd – 26 Nov 1653 (Marriage, St. John Parish)
- Mary Loftus & Thomas Hoy – 26 Apr 1847 (Marriage, St. Mary. Pro Cathedral Parish (RC))

Wedding Witnesses:

Joseph Carr & Margaret Cavanagh

- Mary Loftus & Thomas Wrexam Fitzgerald – 18 Jul 1804 (Marriage, St. Peter Parish)
- Mary Loftus & William Malone
  - o William Malone – b. 1887, bapt. 1887 (Baptism, St. Andrew Parish (RC))

William Malone (father):

Residence - 2 Sandwith Place - 1887

Loftus Surname Ireland: 1600s to 1900s

- Mary Loftus & William Sutton

  o Mary Sutton – b. 1862, bapt. 21 Oct 1862 (Baptism, **SS. Michael & John Parish (RC)**)

William Sutton (father):

Residence - 13 Exchange Street - October 21, 1862

- Nancy Loftus & James Morgan

  o Anne Morgan & Patrick Leonard – 25 Feb 1884 (Marriage, **St. Mary. Pro Cathedral Parish (RC)**)

Anne Morgan (daughter):

Residence - 36 Lower Dorset Street - February 25, 1884

Patrick Leonard, son of Patrick Leonard & Sarah Sharkey (son-in-law):

Residence - 2 St. Lawrence Street - February 25, 1884

Wedding Witnesses:

John Devlin & Mary Devlin

- Olivia Loftus & James O'Connor

  o Harriet Mary O'Connor – b. 22 Feb 1880, bapt. 9 Mar 1880 (Baptism, **St. Agatha Parish (RC)**)

James O'Connor (father):

Residence - 79 North Strand Road - March 9, 1880

Hurst

- Sarah Loftus & John Albert Mons – 24 Aug 1850 (Marriage, **St. Mary. Pro Cathedral Parish (RC)**)

    o   Mary Belinda Mons – bapt. 24 Jul 1854 (Baptism, **Rathmines Parish** (RC))

    o   George William Frederick Mons – bapt. 8 Jul 1855 (Baptism, **Rathmines Parish** (RC))

Wedding Witnesses:

Michael John Ruttle & Julia Mannson

- Susan Loftus & Thomas Foley – 15 Jan 1838 (Marriage, **SS. Michael & John Parish** (RC))

Wedding Witnesses:

John Byrne & Catherine Byrne

- Susanna Loftus & Joseph Ash – 1 Aug 1730 (Marriage, **St. Mary Parish**)
- Unknown Loftus & Unknown Warren – 3 Sep 1788 (Marriage, **St. Mary Parish**)

Unknown Loftus (wife):

Relationship Status at Marriage - widow

Unknown Warren (husband):

Occupation - Reverend Doctor - September 3, 1788

Loftus Surname Ireland: 1600s to 1900s

Name Variations

Includes Latin and Abbreviated forms of names found in the original documents.

Abigail = Abigale, Abigall

Anne = Ann, Anna, Annae

Bartholomew = Barth, Bartholmeus, Bartholomeo

Bridget = Birgis, Brigid, Brigida, Bridgit

Catherine = Catharine, Catharina, Catharinae, Catherina, Cath, Catha, Cathae, Cathe, Cathn, Kate

Charles = Carolus, Charls, Chas

Christopher = Christoph

Daniel = Danielem, Danielis

Edmund = Edmond

Edward = Ed, Edwd

Eleanor = Eleo, Eleonora, Elinor, Ellenor

Elizabeth = Betty, Elisa, Elisabeth, Eliz, Eliza, Elizab, Elizh, Elizth

Ellen = Elena, Ellena

Emily = Emilia

Esther = Essie, Ester

Francis = Fransicum

George = Geo, Georg, Georgius

Grace = Gratiae

Gulielmo = Guil, Guillelmi, Gulielmum, Guillelmus, Gulmi

Helen = Helena

Loftus Surname Ireland: 1600s to 1900s

Honor = Hanora, Honora

James = Jacobi, Jacobus, Jas

Jane = Joanna

Jeanne = Jeannae, Joannae

Joan = Johanna, Joney

John = Jno, Joannem, Joannes, Johannis

Joseph = Jos

Juliana = Julian

Leticia = Letitia, Lettice, Letticia

Lewis = Louis

Luke = Lucas

Margaret = Margarita, Margaritae, Margeret, Marget, Margt

Martha = Marthae

Mary = Maria, My

Mary Anne = Marianna, Marianne, Maryanne

Michael = Michaelis, Michl

Patrick = Pat, Patt, Patk, Patricii, Patricius

Peter = Petri

Richard = Ricardi, Ricardus, Rich, Richd

Robert = Roberti

Rose = Rosa, Rosae

Thomas = Thom, Thomae, Thoms, Thos, Ths

Timothy = Timotheus, Timy

William = Wil, Will, Willm, Wm

Notes

Notes

Notes

Notes

Notes

Notes

Index

K

William
1821 Aug 26 81
1845 Dec 14 81
1856 May 4 73
1860 Jan 8 24
1865 Aug 24 73
1866 Apr 2 5
1868 15
William Valentine
1834 Dec 25 61

Births
Adam
1854 84
Albert George
1872 Sep 8 3
Alice
1851 Nov 26 43
1872 Dec 26 24
Alice Evelyn
1899 Jul 22 42
Amelia Alice
1864 Aug 21 62
Anne
1755 84
1760 May 30 83
1796 84
1835 84
1839 Sep 27 64
1841 Jun 20 53
1850 Jun 8 81
1854 Apr 15 22
1881 Jan 2 64
1893 Sep 27 74
Anne Jane
1860 Jan 24 16
Anne Mary
1846 46
Benjamin
1874 15
Bridget
1877 5
Catherine
1854 Apr 29 43
Catherine Mary

1886 Sep 23 20
Charlotte
1859 May 1 56
Christine
1879 Jan 5 19
Christine Bridget
1885 Dec 23 37
David
1881 Oct 11 37
Dennis
1865 Jun 25 56
Dudley
1746 May 22 57
Edward
1871 15
Elizabeth
1814 85
1850 Jun 30 42
1862 Sep 29 49
Elizabeth Cooper
1819 44
Ellen
1827 Aug 2 72
1828 Apr 3 81
Emily
1867 Aug 21 62
Emily Georgina
1896 May 17 65
Esther Anne
1878 5
Florence Susan
1901 74
Frances
1864 15
Frances Eleanor
1840 May 29 65
Harriet Augusta
1897 Mar 25 74
Henry
1709 Nov 18 37
Henry George
1860 May 21 12
James
1828 Jan 86

Loftus Surname Ireland: 1600s to 1900s

Loftus Surname Ireland: 1600s to 1900s

Loftus Surname Ireland: 1600s to 1900s

About The Author

Donovan Hurst graduated from San Diego State University with a Bachelor of Arts in the major field of studies of History and a minor in the field of studies of Anthropology. He is a current member of The General Society of Mayflower Descendants and has been conducting genealogical research for over 10 years tracing back his ancestors to their ancestral homelands in Denmark, England, France, Germany, Ireland, Norway, and Scotland.

www.ingramcontent.com/pod-product-compliance
Lightning Source LLC
Chambersburg PA
CBHW081154270326
41930CB00014B/3155